# A Leader's Guide to
# Real Jobs
# Real Stories

## Stories by Teens About Succeeding at Work

By Development Without Limit
and Youth Communication

*True Stories by Teens*

# Real Jobs
# Real Stories

### Executive Editors

Eric Gurna and Keith Hefner

### Writers

Andrea Kamins, Sam Quiah, Rebecca Fabiano, Eric Gurna,
Keith Hefner, and Laura Longhine

### Layout & Design

Efrain Reyes, Jr. and Jeff Faerber

### Cover Art

YC Art Dept.

For reprint information, please contact Youth Communication.

ISBN 978-1-933939-97-1

First Edition
Printed in the United States of America

Youth Communication ®
New York, New York
www.youthcomm.org

*Acknowledgments*

Thank you to the Heckscher Foundation and Atlantic Philanthropies for providing the financial support that enabled us to launch the Real Jobs project.

The New York City Department of Youth and Community Development was gracious in providing sites to pilot the program. We appreciate all of the support from staff and teens at the Police Athletic League and the Children's Aid Society.

Many other funders supported the teen training and publishing work at Youth Communication that made this project possible. For example, to produce the *Real Jobs* anthology, we sifted through more than 200 teen-written stories to find 33 that provided a rich and effective mix of stories about work and related experiences. We also selected the illustrations from among hundreds produced over many years by teens in our illustration program. Without that archive of high-quality materials, it would be impossible to create a program like *Real Jobs*. And without generous, long-term support of our youth development and publishing work, that archive would not exist.

Thank you to the following foundations and corporations which have provided that ongoing support: the Altman Foundation, the Robert Bowne Foundation, the Child Welfare Fund, the Clark Foundation, the Ira W. DeCamp Foundation, the Charles Hayden Foundation, the Jenesis Foundation, the Marion Moore Foundation, the New York Community Trust, the Open Society Institute, the Pinkerton Foundation, the Spunk Fund, the W. Clement and Jesse E. Stone Foundation, the Surdna Foundation, Time Warner, and the van Ameringen Foundation. The contributions of many individual donors have also made this work possible. We are extremely grateful to all of these contributors.

# Table of Contents

## Contents

## 4. Health: Manage Stress to Succeed

## 5. College: You Can Do It. Here's How

# Contents

# PART I
## How to Use the Stories With Groups

# Introduction to the Real Jobs Program

*Real Jobs, Real Stories* is a work readiness program for teens.* It has four components:
- an anthology of true stories by teens about work and related experiences
- a workbook for teens
- a leader's guide (the book you're holding) with experiential activities
- professional development in how to implement the program with teens.

*Real Jobs* can be used to help prepare young people for working, to strengthen the skills of teens already on the job, and to help prepare teens for success in managing their lives outside of work. Chapters 1, 2, 6, and 7 focus on job-specific skills, including handling the first day on the job, working with colleagues, developing a professional attitude and approach, exploring careers, and reflecting on the work experience. Chapters 3, 4, and 5 focus on complementary topics: how to manage and save money, how to manage stress, and how to explore options for the future, including higher education.

If teens ask why a work readiness program includes chapters on money, stress, and college, you may want to explain that success on the job is not an isolated event. Long-term career success is directly related to good financial management, good health, and improving one's skills through advanced training.

The *Real Jobs* program is designed to be used in seven three-hour workshops. However, each workshop consists of many discrete activities. With a little planning, you can break each workshop into two 90-minute workshops, or even three one-hour workshops. You can also extend the number of workshops by taking more time with the activities and going deeper in the discussions.

In reviewing the materials, note that the anthology includes 33 stories by teens about work experiences. Only seven of the stories are paired with activities in the workshops. One feature of the *Real Jobs* program is that it gently encourages teens to get in the habit of reading on their own—an essential skill for success in all but the lowest-level jobs, and for success in school.

We encourage you to announce to the teens that there are many more stories in the anthology than you will be covering in the workshop. They are free to read the other stories on their own and will probably find them interesting and helpful in getting and keeping jobs because the stories are by teens just like them.

For example, the last chapter of the anthology includes stories by teens about working in many different jobs and settings, including retail, fast food, child care, hospitals, and more. Because the stories are by peers and focus on very practical experiences, they are especially compelling, even for teens who are ordinarily resistant to reading.

---

* *Real Jobs* can be used with teens and young adults in middle school and high school. It can also be used with young adults, ages 18-24, in a work readiness training program, with slight adjustments to a few activities. For example, the college calendar in session 5 is based on typical activities for high school juniors and seniors. If you are working with older youth you can adjust it to their college or other post-secondary training goals and opportunities.

Also note that throughout the program we interchangeably refer to the young people as teens, students, and participants. If you're working with young adults, or out-of-school youth, please use the terms that work for your group.

Finally, you will notice that many of the lessons in the program require teens to complete short worksheets. Teens, especially in out-of-school settings, may be resistant to worksheets, which remind them of busywork in school. However, they will soon see that these worksheets are tied directly to the fun experiential activities. (The worksheets also help reinforce basic writing skills and they support record-keeping and reflection skills, all of which are helpful on the job.)

The lessons also involve moving around the room and interacting with other participants in games, role plays, and other experiential activities. These help teens build the soft skills they need to succeed on the job, and they're fun. Good luck using this program. And have fun!

## Leaders: What's in It for You?

If you facilitate the activities in this program or any of the other Real Stories programs (see p. 145) you will become more knowledgeable about youth development and will improve your skills in leading groups.

Each workshop also includes multiple activities, so you will increase your experience facilitating many types of activities. These are transferable skills that are useful in any kind of youth work or teaching, and in the corporate world.

If you successfully lead teens through Real Jobs, you will have run a sophisticated work readiness program that involves reading, discussion, writing, managing groups, and facilitating a wide range of experiential activities. You may want to note that on your next application for a job, internship, or college.

Most importantly, because this program consists of effective stories and activities, you will gain the satisfaction of helping teens improve their knowledge of work and the skills they need to get and keep jobs.

For people who are new to the field or would like to strengthen their facilitation skills, we have provided a wealth of helpful information about running groups later in this section.

## Why Use Stories by Teens?

The most powerful influence on adolescents is their peers. They turn to each other for advice on everything from fashion to dating to how to cope with traumatic events. But peer advice raises two challenges. The first is that much of it occurs outside of adult knowledge or supervision. Teens don't generally share their struggles with adults, especially not in adult-led group discussions.

In addition, the quality of peer advice is mixed. There is a good reason why peer pressure—though it can be constructive—has a decidedly mixed reputation.

Youth Communication's true stories by teens help address both of those challenges. Reading and talking about the stories, under the guidance of an adult facilitator, is a particularly effective educational strategy. And because the stories have been carefully edited, they include accurate information and show teens taking effective and appropriate action to learn new skills, develop more constructive attitudes, and manage the challenges in their lives.

The stories also work well because talking about the issues in the stories often feels safer to young people than talking about those same issues in their own lives. Discussing a story by a peer allows for some personal distance. Young people can grapple with the issue in the story in a deep and meaningful way while revealing as much or as little personal information as they choose. For example, when students read Marsha Dupiton's story, "Rewriting My Dream," about the conflict between her goals and her parents' goals for her, some of them may be facing similar conflicts. But even if they're not ready to talk about their situation, they can still explore the issues by talking about Marsha's choices.

Or a student who has an anger problem can read and discuss "Karate Killed the Monster Inside Me" and explore the ways Robin Chan dealt with his anger. Whether teens talk about themselves or talk only about the writers, the discussion will give them valuable new tools and insights, help them feel more capable, and give them specific strategies for meeting the challenges in their lives.

# How to Use This Book and the Lessons

The Leader's Guide contains complete instructions for facilitating the seven workshops in the *Real Jobs* program, including the stories with suggested questions, activities, and student workbook pages and handouts. The workshops follow a consistent four-part format:

1) An opening icebreaker
2) Reading the story aloud with discussion
3) Several experiential activities
4) A closing question

Before you meet with the teens try to review the lessons. Following are the key steps.

## Review the story and workshop summary

This will give you a quick overview of the focus of each workshop, including the youth development goals.

## Read the story

This will give you a clear idea of the story's theme and content. (If possible, read the story out loud to yourself so you'll have a feel for how it sounds and whether there are points that may be difficult or confusing for your students.)

## Check to be sure you have the materials

Most of the lessons require only basic classroom materials: pencils, paper, markers, scissors, a blackboard or flip chart, and tape. But check to see that you have what you need. Also be sure to make photocopies of any materials (provided in this guide) in advance. Making copies is required for activities in sessions 2, 3, 5, and 7. If getting access to a copier is hard in your school or program you may want to make copies for all of those sessions at once.

## Familiarize yourself with the structure and content of the activities

Here are brief descriptions of the four parts of each session, and how to prepare.

- **Opening Icebreaker:** A short activity designed to get teens thinking about the topic.

These are simple activities, but note that some of them require props, including Post-It notes (or paper and tape), chart paper, pennies, and M&Ms. Be sure to read the "Story & Workshop Summary" with each activity at least a day before so you can round up the needed materials. (Though if you find yourself without the needed materials, it's possible to improvise.)

- **Read the Story and Talk About It:** In the Leader's Guide, each story includes suggested discussion questions in the margins. Consider asking these questions. Reading them to yourself in advance and anticipating your students' responses can make the questions seem more natural and less school-like. Note that most of the questions are discussion prompts—with no right or wrong answer. That relieves both you and the teens of the pressure to "know" the answer. Your goal is not to find the right answers. It's to prompt a rich discussion.

Feel free to modify or eliminate these and add your own questions. They are truly just suggested questions. (See "Who Should Read?" [p. 13], and "Avoid the Veiled Quiz," [p. 18], for more thoughts on the read-aloud.)

- **Experiential Activities:** The teens will participate in activity sessions and talk about what they do. Review each activity and imagine how your group will respond. Is it a role play? A social barometer? A competition? Imagine how it will play out with your group. Are they enthusiastic or shy about performing role plays? Are there participants who should not be in the same small group? Any thought you can give to the best way to organize the group will be helpful.

• **Closing Activity:** You'll go around the room, and each participant will answer a closing question designed to reinforce a key theme or insight in the story. Take a look: Will the question work for you or do you want to ask something else or close in a different way? The important thing is to bring the session to a clear end in a way that reinforces what the teens have learned.

This may seem like a lot of preparation time, but you can read the story to yourself and skim the lesson in about 15 minutes. And since all of the lessons follow the same format, and many of the activities, like freewriting, repeat from lesson to lesson, you'll quickly get the hang of the format and activities.

## Do I Have to Do All of the Activities?

We include several activities for each session—possibly more activities than you will have time for. You are the best judge of your group. Review the activities beforehand and select the ones that you think will meet your goals, interest your group, and fit your time frame. Though it is possible to run each session in three hours, including breaks, you could also break up most of the sessions into four or even five one-hour workshops.

**If you have less than three hours per session, here's how to cut it down:** Do the opening activity, read and discuss the story, and do the closing activity. That should take about an hour. If you have more time, add in the experiential activities that will work best with your group, in your time frame.

## Do I Have to Follow the Times?

The time suggested for each activity is merely a recommendation. Some activities may take less time. If you get a good discussion going, an activity could take much longer. If you think some of the activities are especially important for your group, keep your eye on the clock and make sure to include them. But even if you are running out of time, allow five minutes at the end of each session to do the closing activity to provide a sense of closure to the session.

Remember: If discussion is so good on some activities that you cannot get to all of them, that is a sign of success.

# Crib Sheet to the Activities

Each activity in the program has a title, like "Feelings About Your First Day on the Job." We also note the type of experiential activity you will be doing with the teens to give you a quick heads up. Here are the major activities in the program and a brief description of each.

**Brainstorm:** Free-form discussion on a topic

**Charting:** Using chart paper or the board to record teens' ideas

**Debrief:** A brief discussion reflecting on the previous activity or story

**Discussion:** More focused whole group or small group discussion

**Drawing:** Drawing activities (that do not require any drawing talent)

**Freewriting:** Writing without stopping for a brief time to get ideas flowing

**Graffiti wall:** Teens write on multiple sheets of chart paper around the room

**Mingle, Mingle, Huddle:** Teens "mingle" as a large group until you give a signal. Then they "huddle" in small groups or pairs to discuss a prompt.

**Pair share:** Teens share ideas in groups of two

**Role plays and skits:** Teens dramatize a conflict or idea (no acting ability needed)

**Share out:** Small groups report back to the full group

**Social Barometer:** Activities in which teens respond to prompts by moving around the room to show what they believe or how they feel about a topic

**Worksheets:** Pages in the workbook that students will write in. There are also some "information sheets" in the workbook that are purely informational, like "Education Pays," p. 21 [Leader's Guide p. 108].

# Who Should Read? A Note on the Read-Aloud

There are three ways to read the stories. Student volunteers can take turns reading them aloud. You can read them aloud to the students. Or students can read them silently (before or during the session).

The most active approach, and the one we recommend in most instances, is to have the students read the stories aloud. It engages them and is good reading practice.

Note that there are small numbers in the margins that break up the story into sections. If you have each student read a section, 5 to 10 students will get to read, and no one will have to read for too long. For particularly weak readers, consider assigning half a section or even just a paragraph. But try to give everyone a chance, and be encouraging and supportive.

You may even want to talk with the group about how important it is to become a strong reader. And explain that they can play an important role in supporting each other, especially the teens who are struggling.

We strongly recommend that you have students read aloud on a voluntary basis only. You might ask the group, "Could I have four volunteers who are willing to read part of the story aloud?" If reading aloud becomes a chore or a requirement, it may discourage some students who want to be part of the group but are uncomfortable reading aloud. Also, when students are forced to read aloud, the anxiety can distract them from paying attention to the story itself.

If you are a very good reader or have dramatic training, you may want to read the stories yourself—at least from time to time. But doing so cuts down on the teens' participation, and it can be hard to stop and ask questions while you are reading.

If you can give teens copies of the anthology to take home, you may want to ask teens to read the stories on their own. Of course, some teens won't do this, so be prepared to have the teens who did the reading provide a summary, or just read it aloud.

# About Freewriting

Many of the workshops in this book include a freewrite because freewriting is a simple technique for helping members of a group make a connection to the story's major themes. However, to use freewriting effectively, you have to explain it carefully so that people who are not used to writing or are embarrassed by their writing skills will realize freewriting has nothing to do with the kind of writing they do in school. Anyone can do it and enjoy it. It doesn't even have to be in English.

Here are some basic guidelines for freewriting. Review these with the teens the first time you use freewriting. Once you've done it a few times, the teens will get an instinctive feel for it.

## The Rules

Correct grammar, spelling, and punctuation do not matter in freewriting. The only rule is to write without stopping. (Writing nonstop frees up emotions and ideas. Since the only requirement is for the writer to keep his or her pen moving, freewriting is not difficult for unskilled or reluctant writers.)

Tell the participants that if they are stuck, they should simply write, "I don't know what to say," over and over, until something occurs to them.

Limit the writing to a brief amount of time, usually 90 seconds, so there's no pressure to write at length, but there is pressure to get some ideas flowing. (It's a good idea to conspicuously look at your watch as you begin so students know you'll really stop on time.)

Sharing is voluntary: To encourage group members to write freely, tell them that they may choose whether or not they want to share what they write.

## The Procedure

Read the freewriting prompt aloud to the group. (You may also write it on the board or flip chart, but it's usually best just to read it aloud. That may seem less school-like to the participants.) Here's a sample prompt:

"Think of a time something bad happened to you, or you were treated unfairly. What happened? Who was to blame? What did you learn from it? How did the experience help you grow or change?"

Feel free to read the prompt a second time so it settles in with students. Also, remind them that it is a prompt. They don't have to literally answer each question if they don't want to. They should just write what comes to mind.

We strongly encourage adult leaders to freewrite along with the group. Writing along with the group can help you understand the feelings the teens are experiencing. Whatever you jot down, even a few short sentences, can illuminate common ground between you and your group. In addition, reluctant group members will be encouraged to write when they see you writing along with them.

Ask a few volunteers to read what they've written or to discuss their feelings about what they've written if they prefer not to reveal specifics. (You may want to read some of your writing, but don't overdo it. The participants' feelings and experiences, not yours, should be the focus.) Sometimes teens may not want to read what they've written, but will allow another teen or the leader to read it to the group. Ask the group to think about what they've written as they begin reading the story.

During the discussion, refer group members back to their freewriting responses. Draw connections between their freewriting and the story's themes.

# About Role Plays

### Goals

The goal of having teens enact role plays is to accentuate the themes of the stories—to make them come alive for the teens, and to give the teens a chance to add their own dramatic twist. There are role plays in sessions 1, 2, 4, and 7.

By introducing the ideas of dramatic conflict and dramatic need, role plays enable teens to connect emotionally with the conflicts and challenges faced by the writers. Role plays can encourage teens to think and act on their feet, loosen up creatively, and become comfortable in front of each other. They can also teach teens the importance of listening carefully and working cooperatively.

Role plays are also a way for teens to practice acting and reacting in new ways. In "Hamlet," Shakespeare declared that theater was like a mirror held up to life. Augusto Boal, a theatre director, activist, and drama theorist said, "I think that's very nice. But I would like to have a mirror with some magic properties in which, if we don't like the image that we have in front of us, it would allow us to penetrate into the mirror and transform our image and then come back with our image transformed." That is the power of role plays—to give young people the chance to practice transforming their own behavior and their understanding of it.

The first time you do a role play, explain that the purpose of the activity is to highlight a theme in the story in a way that is fun and interpreted by the role players. The goal is not great acting. It's just to imagine what the characters would do or say in a particular situation.

Point out that the audience is also part of the role play. They need to pay attention and think about what's happening in the scene. At any time, an audience member may be called upon to step in and give a new interpretation of the conflict.

Role plays can be as short as a minute or as long as the actors can keep the scene going.

### The Rules

No physical contact between actors. Players should follow the role play description, but if one teen introduces an idea or fact into the scene, the others should accept it as reality.

### The Procedure

Read the role play scenario out loud.

Pick volunteers and review their dramatic needs in the scene. In most role plays the characters' needs (what they want) must establish a clear conflict that will drive the action of the role play.

For example, in the "First Impressions" role play (p. 31), the conflict is between the boss, who expects people to do the "right" thing, and the employees, who will demonstrate the "wrong" thing in some of the role plays. When the actors are chosen and the scene is clear, start the role play.

*Tip: The adult leader can actively participate by playing one of the characters. This is an excellent opportunity for the leader to model open, vulnerable behavior for the teens. If they see that you're not afraid to open up and take risks, they will be more inclined to go for it, too.*

Be ready to intervene if the role play is not moving forward or if it's getting out of hand.

When the scene is over, debrief with the group. Ask the audience members what they saw in the role play. Did anything surprise them? Would they have changed any of the responses? How?

## Group Guidelines

Clear group guidelines provide a set of shared expectations about the way group sessions will be run. They let your group know what to expect from you and from each other.

By giving sessions structure and predictability, guidelines help group members feel safe. As a result, teens will be more willing to participate and to benefit from the stories and related activities. You may want to post the guidelines on the wall of your classroom.

We recommend that group members contribute to developing the guidelines. This creates a greater sense of shared responsibility for abiding by them. Even if you already have guidelines in place, you can involve the group in developing additional guidelines or in discussing the existing ones.

Here are some possible guidelines:
• Group members should listen to and respect each other.
• One person speaks at a time.
• Each person has a chance to share thoughts and feelings, but no one has to share.
• Everyone in the group should feel valued and accepted. All points of view are welcome. There are no wrong answers.

# Ten Tips and Tricks for Leading Groups

**1. Keep a log of every youth you work with.** At least once a week, try to write a couple of sentences about what has stood out for you about each student in the group. Include your concerns, but always write at least one sentence on what you like about this young person or a positive quality they have. This is especially important for young people who get under your skin. If you consciously and explicitly write about a positive side or strength in their personality or behavior, that insight will start to seep into your interactions with them, and it will make a huge difference to you, to them, and to your group (see tip #5).

*Review your log* right before the next class, at least until you feel you have gotten to know the students pretty well.

**2. Build and maintain trust by recognizing young people for their contributions.**
Remember: young people crave recognition and hate humiliation (just like the rest of us, only more so). When students deserve recognition, give it freely.

*Be affirming.* In many discussions, you will find students making thoughtful or creative contributions that never occurred to you. Reflect those contributions back to them. ("Wow, I didn't realize that students were being bullied at the bus stop. Has anyone else had that experience?") Let them know that when they put their minds to something (such as a problem with a supervisor, or a conflict with a coworker) they may know even better than adults how to solve it.

*Give special roles.* The activities in this guide provide lots of opportunities to give students special "jobs" that allow them to contribute and to see their contributions recognized (for example, recording responses on chart paper or being a group spokesperson). This can be particularly use-ful if you have a student who is disruptive, to help refocus his or her energy in a more positive direction. Remember that "troublemakers" are often leaders in disguise. Giving them a role, such as leading an activity with you, can tap their leadership skills, and put them in the position of managing group behavior.

**3. Build and maintain trust by managing conflicts respectfully.** If a student does something in class that requires a reprimand, note the inappropriate activity (so the class knows that you won't let it slide), but talk to the student privately, after class, about the specifics. For minor misbehaviors, like talking, remind the whole group about your group guidelines and expectations instead of singling a student out.

For example: "Remember, when everyone speaks at the same time, it is difficult to hear what anyone has to say, so let's try to keep our 'one mic' rule."

*Ask, don't tell.* When talking to students about a conflict, ask students what happened, their perception of why it happened, how they feel about it, and how they can use that information next time or to solve the problem now.

For example: "Why do you think that person was upset about the comment you made during group? What could you do differently next time?"

**4. Don't feel you have to know everything or solve every problem.** The ultimate "content" of these lessons is the students' experiences and perceptions, and how they they can use them to become more effective on the job. Since they are the experts on their own lives, your role is more trusted guide than expert. When the group is discussing how to deal with a challenging situation, like the conflict between Marsha Dupiton's goals for herself and those her parents have for her, you simply cannot assume you know the answer (or even what the problem is). Unlike subject area classes, there are few right answers.

That can feel disconcerting, but as you get comfortable, it can also be very exciting. If students see that you take delight in learning from them and in their often-creative responses to the challenges they face, you will actually have more influence with them.

**5. Monitor your reactions to the most difficult students.** How you respond to the difficult students can set a tone for the entire class. Students will watch your interactions with their peers very closely in deciding how to behave themselves—including how supportive they will be toward you.

When you begin working with a new group, it is worth devoting extra time and energy early on to thinking about how to respond to the most challenging students. Your skill and compassion in handling them is a litmus test for the other young people: the better you perform, the more they will trust and respect you.

**6. Be nonjudgmental.** Nothing will cause young people to clam up faster than the feeling that they are being judged. For example, when teens say that their ideal job is rap star or professional athlete, don't tell them that those goals are unrealistic. Instead, ask what appeals to them about those careers. Ask if they know about any of the other jobs in the music industry or the sports industry. For every star musician or athlete, there are thousands of support staff who do everything from audio engineering to sports psychology. By being nonjudgmental, you can help teens become more open to other careers in their general area of interest. Here are two strategies for being nonjudgmental:

*Trust in the values in the stories.* Youth Communication stories are carefully designed to promote positive values. However, they also acknowledge negative values and bad choices, so those may come up in conversation. Our experience in teaching hundreds of stories is that the good values win out in the end. So don't get freaked out if some negative ideas pop up early in the story or in discussion. They will get resolved by the end.

*Use the power of the group.* If one student makes an outrageous comment, instead of reprimanding him, ask mildly, "Does anyone else have another opinion on this topic?" Nine times out of ten, another student will present a contrary view—which will be much more powerful than your doing so.

**7. Show that you're listening to and aware of everyone in the group.** When participants are speaking, make eye contact, don't interrupt, and give signs of listening like nodding and using encouraging phrases such as "uh-huh" and "yeah." Also, make sure you understand what someone is feeling and saying by restating comments (paraphrasing) or asking for clarification.

*Use stacking.* When several participants wish to speak at once, it is useful to "stack" them by simply calling on one participant and then saying who will speak next and who will speak after that. When people know their desire to participate has been acknowledged, they can relax and listen while they wait their turn.

**8. Avoid the veiled quiz.** When you are leading discussions, you want to avoid the "veiled quiz." The veiled quiz is asking a question that you already know the answer to, getting a response from teens, and pretending that it's a discussion.

The veiled quiz is common in school, where teachers want to check in with students to see if they have learned the material. There's nothing wrong with it as long as it doesn't masquerade as a real discussion. But in the *Real Jobs* program, the goal is to spark a discussion—to get the teens engaged—not to quiz teens on what they know.

For example, in a veiled quiz, the teacher or leader asks questions to find out whether the students remember certain points of the story's plot or aspects of the characters. Questions like:

"When Julio cut school, where did he go instead?"
   *or*
"What are Rose's favorite places to go when she feels sad?"

Veiled quiz questions tend to have answers that are either correct or incorrect. They feel like school, and in an out-of-school-time setting, they can shut down discussion. Instead, try asking open-ended questions that encourage participants to think about how they feel about the issues raised in the story, or how the ideas relate to their own lives. Questions like:

"Why do you think Julio cut school? Do you think his reasons were valid?"
   *or*
"In the story, Rose has places she likes to go when she is sad. What are the places you go when you feel a particular way—happy, sad, or otherwise?"

The veiled quiz method of leading a "discussion" is so common that it can take some practice to break the habit. But when you do, you'll know right away because instead of students holding back and trying to figure out what you want, they will be jumping into the discussion and telling you what they know.

**9. Challenge teens to think deeply.** After asking a question of the group, wait several seconds before accepting answers; this eliminates competition to be first with an answer and allows all participants to assimilate the question and consider a response. For those times when participants are reluctant to speak, waiting patiently is more useful than filling the silence with the sound of your own voice.

*Ask follow-up questions.* You can also help participants explore and expand their ideas and feelings by asking open-ended follow-up questions. You can ask participants to give examples of personal stories that illuminate the topic under discussion, compare and connect ideas, or simply say a little more about the topic.

*Play devil's advocate.* Don't be afraid to raise issues that are contrary to what you or your students might expect (even unpopular or "politically incorrect" views). This helps the group consider more options, and it helps you avoid being pigeonholed as someone who always responds in a predictable way.

**10. Go with the flow.** The lessons in this manual provide a framework for helping young people explore their lives and imagine constructive solutions to their challenges. Unlike academic lessons, you do not have to complete all of these to be successful. If the opening activity in one of these lessons sparks a 20-minute conversation (which means that you won't finish the rest of the lesson), that is a *success*, not a failure. If the lesson is working so well that you want to continue it in the next session, feel free to do so.

## *Facilitation Troubleshooting*

| PROBLEM | ASK YOURSELF... | TRY... |
|---|---|---|
| Everybody talking | Is it because they are so interested? | Ask them to tell their idea to a partner. |
| | Is it because they are not interested? | Rephrase the question, or add interest to the topic, or drop it. |
| | Is it because they have not heard the question? | Get their attention first, check your timing, review the ground rules, etc. |
| Nobody talking | Do they understand? | Rephrase the question. Give more information. |
| | Are they interested? | Clarify the topic or question and challenge them to consider it. |
| | Do they need to think more to formulate their ideas? | Wait! Give them time to think. You may also invite them to discuss the question with a partner or write individually about it. |
| | Are they comfortable? | Help them get to know you and each other better by playing icebreaker games. |
| Side conversations or interference | Is the discussion hitting too close to home? | Give participants time to write individually about the topic, or table the discussion. Remind teens they don't have to reveal personal information. |
| | Is the discussion of no concern to them? | Acknowledge the fact, and shorten the discussion, if possible. |
| Shocking or "funny" statements | Is it really in order to get attention? Or could it be a method to cover up feeling embarrassed? | Deal with this directly. Keep your sense of humor! Sometimes you may decide to have a private talk with the individual(s) involved, particularly if this is a pattern. |
| | Is it from an inability to express themselves clearly? | Rephrase by asking, "Do you mean...?" Or ask them to rephrase—and give them some time. |
| Someone too disruptive to stay in the group | How can I stop the behavior and not build resentment? How can I help the person take responsibility for his or her own behavior? | Ask the person to leave the group until she or he is able to return without being disruptive. Consider giving the person a leadership role. |

This section is adapted from *Ways We Want Our Class To Be*,
a publication of the Developmental Studies Center (Oakland, CA, 1996).

# PART II

## The Workshop Sessions

# SESSION 1: ORIENTATION

## Getting to Know Your Job
## and Your Colleagues

# Rush Hour at Macy's

## Story & Workshop Summary

**Time:** 180 minutes (including one 15-minute break)

**Materials:** chart paper, markers, "good idea" and "bad idea" signs, pens

**Story:** Rush Hour at Macy's

**Core Emotions:** self-doubt, confidence, relief

**Theme:** Every job has challenges, and it's important not to get discouraged when things go wrong.

**Plot:** The writer faces impatient customers, an uncooperative cash register, and self-doubt during his first day at work. But with a little help from a colleague and his own resilience, he proves he can do the job.

**Youth Development Goals:**
• Young people will increase their understanding of the benefits of working.
• Young people will be able to articulate the importance of establishing and maintaining positive relationships with coworkers.
• Young people will learn how to make a good first impression at work and will understand why first impressions matter.

**Note:** *It is a good idea to set group guidelines at the beginning of the session. See p. 16 for tips on how to establish group guidelines.*

**Tip:** *This session emphasizes the importance of making a positive first impression. The facilitator should model this behavior by shaking participants' hands and greeting them with a smile when they enter the room. It will set a professional tone.*

## Opening Icebreaker

**Mingle, Mingle, Huddle!** (15 min)

Tell participants that you are going to say, "Mingle, Mingle!" When you do, they are to walk around the room saying hello and introducing themselves to one another. When you say, "Huddle," they should form groups of three or four and discuss the question you give them for a minute or two. When time is up, say, "Mingle," and repeat this process.

**Questions:**

• For the first huddle: What are some reasons people work?
• For the second huddle: What do you like about your current job? Or, what kind of job would you like to have?
• For the third huddle: What are some of the challenges of your current job? Or, what do you think would be challenging about working?

After the third huddle, bring the full group back together to discuss.

**Debrief:**

• Are you used to going up to people and introducing yourself?
• Is it harder in "real life" situations like school or work?
• What makes it easier to meet people?

Explain that this activity helped participants get to know one another, and that they'll get to know many more people on the job, like bosses, coworkers, clients, customers, and others. Ask: "Why is it important to communicate well and make a good first impression at work?"

## Activity: Feelings About Your First Day on the Job
**graffiti wall** (15 min)

Write each of the following sentence starters at the top of a sheet of chart paper and post them around the room with some markers near each:
- On my first day of work, I was/will be nervous about…
- On my first day of work, I was/will be excited about…
- On my first day of work, some challenges I might face are…
- On my first day of work, I will try to remember…

Give participants a few moments to walk around the room and write their responses. Then review the charts with the large group. Affirm that excitement and apprehension are both normal feelings when beginning a job.

## Read the Story and Talk About It    (20 min)

**Introduce the story:** Tell the class that you are going to read a story about the challenges one young man faced on his first day of work—and how he survived them.

Take turns reading the story. Pause from time to time when there is a passage that you think is ripe for discussion. Ask the suggested questions, and/or ones that you think will be helpful to your group.

Kassaye Selassie

# Rush Hour at Macy's

### By Sharif Berkeley

1.  Imagine you're working at a cash register in a department store, with several people waiting on line with their purchases. Suddenly there's a malfunction with the register and it won't let any transactions go through. The people on line get restless and start to complain.

    You break into a nervous sweat, then you try the transaction again. It still won't go through. Now the line is even longer than before and you still haven't finished with your first customer. You hear people say, "Come on already," and, "Damn, he's slow," but of course they don't understand that it's your first day at work and the faulty computer isn't making it any better.

    Could you see this as your first day on the job? This is exactly how it went for me on my first day at Macy's.

    I had wanted to work at Macy's for the longest time, and when I finally got hired I thought it was going to be a wonderful

    11

**REAL JOBS**

experience. But if I knew that the first day was going to be that hectic, I would have paid more attention in the 15-hour training course.

2. **My Register Breaks at Rush Hour**

My employer had placed me in electronics at first because I'm an expert in that field, but there was so much confusion between the employees and the management that I had to be placed in housewares, in the Macy's Cellar.

That put a damper on my enthusiasm because I knew nothing about pots, pans, and all that house stuff. To top it off, I was stationed right next to the clearance sale area, where people were running around grabbing up things like they were possessed by shopping demons. It was like being thrown into a lion's cage after being marinated in A.1. steak sauce.

> **It was like being thrown into a lion's cage after being marinated in A.1. steak sauce.**

It was a little past 5 o'clock, and I was unfortunately caught up in the shopping rush hour. I thought that I had remembered all the instructions in the training course, but little did I know that when you get nervous you forget things.

My first customer approached. She had several items in her hands from the clearance area. She dropped her load and I began to scan her items. The first two items came up on the screen. I was halfway done. But the next three items had no price on them. I scanned the UPC symbol, and all three came up as one cent each. This couldn't be right; nothing in Macy's sells for one cent. I asked the other cashiers how much the items really were and they didn't know.

I looked back at my register to see that, by this time, two more people were waiting on line. I called my manager and he said

12

---

**Q.** What do you think Sharif was expecting his first day to be like?

**Q.** What could he have done to be better prepared? Is it the number of hours you spend in training that prepares you for a job or is it something else?

*Welcome to the World of Work*

that the items were 97 cents each. When I came back there were five people waiting on my line. I thought that everything was all right because now I could move on to the next customer with no problem, but I thought too soon.

3. **Starting to Panic**

My first customer had given me a check and—just my luck—my check reader wasn't working. By this time the customers waiting on line were getting irritable and discussing my performance among themselves.

I started to panic. I knew that if the check reader wasn't working I had to enter the sets of numbers on the check manually, but I forgot how! I tried but I entered the numbers in the wrong sequence three times. I was sweating and I felt like the people waiting in line were grim reapers ready to kill me on the spot if I didn't hurry up.

Finally another cashier took pity on me and came over to assist me. The people had been standing in line so long that the manager decided to give them coffee mugs just to calm them down. The cashier standing beside me told them that it was my first day and that I was nervous.

To my amazement, the customers all had a change of face. A lot of them understood the position that I was in and some even said to my manager, "If it's his first day, someone should have been helping him out the whole time."

A few of them came up to me and told me not to feel bad because they could relate to how it felt being my first day. Then and there my wounds of disappointment were covered by a big band-aid of confidence. I didn't think that people still had that much compassion.

During the rest of the day I gradually got the hang of things, thanks to my coworkers, who are still there for me whenever I need help or a price check.

**Q.** WWhy did his coworker choose to help him? Have you ever helped out when a coworker was struggling? (Or, do you think you would?

**Q.** Why is it important to have good relationships with your coworkers? What can you do to ensure that you and your coworkers will get along?

13

REAL JOBS

#### 4. Racking Up Sales

That first day was one I would never forget: the feeling of all eyes on me, people cracking the whip telling me to hurry up, the beads of sweat on my forehead, and the nerve-wracking anxiety. It all made me wish that I had paid attention in the training session.

The nervousness I felt could be compared to being up on stage in front of a crowd for the first time. It's a situation that not many people can handle, but eventually you get used to it.

It's been a long while since my first day and now I've got the hang of everything and I go through customers like water. Not a day goes by without me having over $1,000 in sales. Some of the same customers I saw on my first day come back to shop, say hi, and see that I've gotten better. I even have customers who like to come on my line because I treat them better than some of the other cashiers do.

#### 5. Don't Doubt Yourself

The first day on any job can be hectic, whether it's dealing with customers or a job where your boss is constantly looking over your shoulder.

My advice is to be persistent and don't doubt yourself. Even though some people may look down on you because you're new, don't give them any excuse to believe what they think of you. Do your job to the best of your ability.

My job is very rewarding, although the first day was rough. But that's what it took to get better and faster at what I do, and with the help of my coworkers, friendly customers, and a fat check on Fridays, I guess it's all worthwhile.

---

*Sharif was 15 when he wrote this story. He later graduated from high school, attended Lehman College, and worked in computer sales.*

14

# Explore the Ideas

### Discussion: What's My Motivation?
(10 min)

Ask the Group:
- Besides the money, what do you think made the job worthwhile for Sharif?
- How would it feel to work at a job where money is your only motivation?
- What other factors would make a job feel worthwhile to you?

### Activity 1: What's in It for Me?
### worksheet, pair share, discussion (20 min)

Ask participants to work with a partner to complete the worksheet on p. 3, "What's in It for Me?" [Leader's Guide p. 34]. They will go through the story and list the benefits to *the author* of having his job. Then, they will circle the benefits on the list that also apply to *them*.

Finally, they will create a list of benefits they hope to get from *their job*, such as learning to work with people from different backgrounds, or improving their punctuality. Give the pairs about 10 minutes to work on this.

When time is up, ask the pairs to share with the large group. First, discuss the benefits to Sharif. Then ask participants to share the benefits they expect to gain from their own work experience. If they aren't mentioned, be sure to elicit benefits like:
- experience to put on a resume
- making friends
- building skills like typing, filing, copying, or working with groups
- developing patience (especially for those working with children or in customer service)
- building relationships with coworkers and employers who may help them in the future (networking)
- learning about themselves (what they like and don't like, what they're good at).

### Break (15 min)

### Activity 2: First Impressions
### discussion, worksheet, role play (40 min)

Write the following quote from philosopher William James on a flip chart:

*"It is our attitude at the beginning of a difficult task which, more than anything else, will affect its successful outcome." –William James*

Ask participants what they think the quote means.

Elicit that in order to have the most successful work experience possible, it's important to start with a good attitude and to set goals to help us learn new things and acquire new skills. If you start your job believing that it will be terrible, you'll probably prove yourself right.

Ask: "Why is it important to make a good first impression? What happens if you get off on the wrong foot?"

Break participants into groups of four and distribute blank paper or sheets of chart paper. Tell the groups that they have five minutes to think of the "Top Five" mistakes they think people make that give a *bad* first impression.

When time is up, ask them to turn over the page and give them five more minutes to write at least five ways to make a *good* first impression.

Then tell the groups their task is to role play all five items on each list. Give the groups about 10 minutes to prepare. They should create a scene set in a workplace where two new employees are starting their first day of work. One group member should portray all of the "dos" and another group member should portray all of the "don'ts." Other group members can play the boss, coworkers, etc.

Give each group a chance to present. After each presentation ask the audience to identify the dos and don'ts that were shown.

*Tip: If you are running short on time or you have a very large group, you can just have a couple of groups present and then move on.*

After each group has presented, review and discuss "Tips for Making a Positive First Impression" on p. 4 in the workbook [Leader's Guide p. 35]. Ask the teens if they agree with the tips. Which ones do they think are most important? Hardest to do? Why?

## Activity 3: Good Idea, Bad Idea
### social barometer, discussion (20 min)

Explain that every job has benefits as well as challenges. Ask participants for examples of what went wrong for Sharif in the story and how he handled it.

Next, ask everyone to stand in the center of the room. On one side of the room, post a sign that says "good idea" and on the other side a sign that says "bad idea."

Tell students that you're going to read some scenarios. Ask them to react to the scenarios by standing on the side of the room that corresponds to whether they think the action was a good idea or a bad idea. Or they can stay in the middle of the room if they are neutral or unsure.

After each scenario, ask participants to explain their position. Ask the people on the "bad idea" side to suggest alternatives for how the characters in the scenario could have responded.

*Note: There are no absolute right or wrong answers to these questions. The teens' reasons for their answers are far more important than the position they take. Try to foster a full and open discussion in which teens really wrestle with these difficult decisions.*

*Tip: You could have a teen read each of the scenarios instead. This would enable you to participate with the teens in the activity, and play "devil's advocate" in the event that all of the teens end up standing on the same side of the room.*

SCENARIO 1: It's the first day of Brenda's new job. For some reason, her alarm clock doesn't go off, so she wakes up late and has to rush to get ready. She had planned to iron her shirt before leaving for work, but it would make her late if she took the time to do it now. She throws on her wrinkled shirt and runs out the door so that she'll make it to work on time.

SCENARIO 2: It's Jon's first day on the job and he really likes his coworkers so far. After they all take their lunch break together, one coworker pulls Jon aside and starts gossiping about the rest of the group. Later, Jon decides to pull his other coworkers aside to warn them about the gossiper.

SCENARIO 3: Carlos arrives for his first day at work at a retail store. He is ringing up a customer when she starts complaining about the price of an item. She complains that he is trying to charge her too much and demands that he give her a huge discount. His supervisor is on a lunch break and won't be back for an hour, so he has to make a decision about what to do on his own. He remembers his supervisor saying, "The customer is always right," so Carlos decides to give her the discount even though it means the store will lose some money.

**Activity 4: Me Shield**

**worksheet, pair share** (20 min)

Ask participants to fill out the Me Shield worksheet on p. 5 [Leader's Guide p. 36]. After a few minutes, ask everyone to find a partner and share what they wrote. Allow volunteers to share responses to each question with the larger group. (If you like, you can explain that a shield or coat of arms is a traditional way to show your values and beliefs.)

## Closing Activity (5 min)

Ask each participant to complete this sentence: **"My biggest goal for my work experience is…"**

# What's in It for Me?

*The Benefits of Working*

In the story "Rush Hour at Macy's," the author, Sharif, faces some major challenges. He also points out some of the benefits of his job. In the space below, list all of the benefits you can think of that Sharif will get from his job. You can look back at the story to help you remember.

_____

_____

_____

_____

_____

_____

_____

_____

Now look at the list above and CIRCLE all the benefits you listed for Sharif that apply to *you* as you work at your current job.

Then think of up to five additional benefits that you will get from your job. List them below.

1. _____

2. _____

3. _____

4. _____

5. _____

# Tips for Making a Positive First Impression

Your supervisor and your colleagues will make assumptions about you based on their first impression, so think carefully about the impression you make and how it will help you achieve your goals on the job. Here are some things that contribute to a good first impression.

## Be On Time!

If you are late to work even once during your first week or two, you could show up on time every day for the next year and people will still think you are the kind of person who is late. Make it a habit to arrive early, especially for the first couple weeks on the job.

## Ask Questions & Take Initiative

What's the one thing that supervisors hate most? It's employees who don't ask questions or take initiative. If you aren't sure about something, don't wait until your supervisor has to explain it to you. Ask! And whenever you don't have anything to do, volunteer to do something helpful. For example, if there's an event planned in the cafeteria, volunteer to set up the chairs and tables.

## Have a Positive Attitude

They call it "work" for a reason. You often have to do things that may be unpleasant, feel "beneath you," or are just tedious. Remember, you're going to be there anyway. It's easier on you—and everyone else—to do an unpleasant task with a good attitude than a bad one.

## Use Positive Body Language

Especially at first, you will be judged as much by your body language as by what you say. The most important words in body language are "eye contact" and "posture." People who are successful look other people in the eye when talking to them. They also sit and stand straight instead of slouching, so they look alert and ready to go. Both of these skills can take practice, but the better you get at them, the better the reaction you'll get from others and the more successful you'll become.

## Dress Appropriately

Know the dress code at your job and follow it (even if it's not written down). If you're at a summer camp, you may be allowed to wear shorts and a t-shirt. If you're working in an office, you may have to wear a collared shirt and slacks—or maybe even a coat and a tie. While there are variations within the dress code (unless you're required to wear a uniform), they can be quite narrow. You may think there's nothing wrong with wearing a tank top or a t-shirt to work, but if not one of your supervisors wears one, don't do it.

In addition, regardless of the job, make sure you're well-groomed: comb your hair, make sure your nails are clean, don't overdo it on cologne or perfume, and keep your jewelry modest.

## Learn Names

Here's a secret to success: Learn the name of everyone you work with and use it when you talk with them. If you talk to a very successful person, they will often tell you that a key to their success was developing a method to remember people's names. You would be surprised how many of them go home at night and write down the name of everyone they met, along with one memorable thing about the person that helps them remember the name.

If that seems goofy to you, just know that someone else is doing it, and someday you may be competing with that person for a job. You won't even know their name, but they'll know yours.

35

# Me Shield

3 responsibilities I will have in my job:

_____

_____

_____

Skills I have that will help me succeed at my job:

_____

_____

_____

Skills I want to develop:

_____

_____

_____

3 resources available to help me succeed at my job:

_____

_____

_____

# SESSION 2: WORK READINESS

## Becoming More Professional

# Quiet on the Job

## Story & Workshop Summary

**Time:** 180 minutes (including one 15-minute break)

**Materials:** chart paper, markers, pens, photocopies of cards for the Communication Styles Meet and Greet activity (enough so that each participant has one slip with one of the words on it)

**Story:** Quiet on the Job

**Core Emotions:** frustration, feeling misunderstood, self-consciousness

**Theme:** Success at work often requires developing—or enhancing—personality traits that may be difficult or challenging.

**Plot:** Danielle is quiet and self-conscious at work. She feels misunderstood and frustrated when people criticize her for being this way.

### Youth Development Goals:
• Young people will be able to define what it means to be "professional" and to identify some "soft skills" that are important in the workplace.
• Young people will identify which of these qualities they already possess and how they could work on developing others.
• Young people will have an increased understanding of the importance of time management and will reflect on their own time-management skills.

**Note:** It is a good idea to review group guidelines at the beginning of each session.

## Opening Icebreaker

**A to Z of Professionalism** (15 min)

**A to Z relay**

Break participants into teams of five or six. Have each team line up at charts that have the alphabet written vertically down the page.

*Tip: Prepare the charts in advance. They should look like this:*

| A | N |
|---|---|
| B | O |
| C | P |
| D | Q |
| E | R |
| F | S |
| G | T |
| H | U |
| I | V |
| J | W |
| K | X |
| L | Y |
| M | Z |

One at a time, in the style of a relay race, participants will write a word that comes to mind when they hear the word "professionalism." They will write one word for each letter on the chart. Give some examples by saying, "I think of words like suit, neat, on time, etc." Tell them that team members can help each other out, and that spelling doesn't matter. Explain that all of the responses have to relate somehow to "professionalism" and that teams will have a chance to challenge any words that seem irrelevant.

When everyone is ready, the teams will compete to see who can complete their chart first. Tell them that if they're stumped by the first letter, they can use words where the given letter falls in the middle of the word. For example, for the letter "X" someone might write "flexible."

After the teams complete the activity, allow the groups to examine each other's charts and give each team the opportunity to challenge any items they are unsure of. (Use any challenges to provoke discussion about what traits are and are not involved in professionalism.)

*Tip: Consider imposing a limit of three challenges per chart if the teams start going overboard.*

After reviewing each chart, explain that it can be hard to know exactly what it means to "be professional," but that it basically means behaving in a way that will help you be successful at work. Highlight any especially good examples of professionalism from the charts.

# Read the Story and Talk About It (20 min)

**Introduce the story:** Tell the class that you are going to read a story about a girl whose behavior seems to be limiting her potential to succeed in a job.

Take turns reading the story. Pause from time to time when there is a passage that you think is ripe for discussion. Ask the suggested questions, or add ones that you think will be helpful to your group.

Martell Brown

# Quiet on the Job

**By Danielle Wilson**

1.  I get so mad and offended when teachers and coworkers say about me, "Danielle is a nice girl, but she's so quiet." I get fed up because I don't consider myself quiet at all. When they say that I am, it makes me feel frustrated and completely misunderstood.

    But in a way I understand why they say that. You see, it's almost like there are two different Danielles inside of me. There is the At-Home-Danielle, who chills, laughs, and jokes with her friends. And then there's the At-School-or-Work-Danielle who just goes to work or school to do what she's gotta do and be out.

    I worked as a receptionist in my school, where all I did was answer the phone and say, "Good afternoon, please hold." So there was no one to really talk to. But the truth is, if there was someone to talk to like a boss or a secretary, I wouldn't say much anyway. That's because I don't feel I'd be able to talk to a boss or a coworker like I talk to my friends. I wouldn't know what to say.

    29

**Q.** Why does Danielle think she wouldn't be able to talk to a boss or coworker? What makes communicating at work different than communicating in other situations?

## REAL JOBS

2. **Home Life vs. Professional Life**

I think everyone is a little different when they're at home than when they are in the real world. At home I live with my brother, who's 20, and my sister, who's 16. Between these two I feel like I'm the adult at home. I take care of my sister, pay the bills, and go to school and work.

> I don't really know how to talk with authority figures. So at work or school I just stay quiet.

Even though my brother is older than I am, I've always been more responsible than he is. I sometimes have to tell him what to do, like, "Pick up your trash!" "Wash the dishes!" "Clean your room!" Sometimes I feel like I have two big, grown teenagers to look after who didn't come out of me. Makes you not want to have kids!

My aunt helps me with money, but she lives all the way across town so I don't see her that much.

**Q.** How do you think it makes Danielle feel when people call her "quiet"? Which is the "real" Danielle?

3. **Letting Loose With Friends...**

With my friends I let loose from all the responsibility. I bust out. Like one time, I was with my friend when a guy who had been stalking her knocked on the door. My friend didn't know how to tell him to leave her alone, but I did. I said, "Boy, you better listen and listen good. My friend Tiffany doesn't want you, never has and never will, so leave her alone, please, thank you kindly." Then I slammed the door in his face. When I got back to my room my friends started busting out laughing.

If my teachers or coworkers knew how I act at home, I don't think they'd believe it. They wouldn't say I was quiet at all.

4. **...But Quiet on the Job**

I think part of the reason I'm so different at home is because at home I don't have to answer to any adult or authority figure, except my aunt, "the big boss lady across town," and, well, she's

30

42

*Learning the Culture*

all the way across town. So that means I can stay up as long as I want, have company any time I want, basically eat when I want and wherever I want. It also means I don't really know how to talk with authority figures. So at work or school I just stay quiet. I feel like if I remain quiet no one will notice that I'm there, and they can't tell me what to do.

But being quiet at work doesn't work all the time. It sometimes makes the boss pick on you more. When I was working at Pretzel Time, I had to give out samples of pretzels outside of the store to try to get customers to come in. The other people who worked there would stand out with the samples while talking to people passing by and laughing with them. They would do practically anything to get those people to come into the store.

But when it was my turn, I was quiet. All I would do is stand there and shout, "Free samples!" I got a lot of greedy people taking the samples, but almost no one walking into the store. My boss criticized me for that.

**Q.** Do you agree that the boss was picking on her, or is he right that she's not doing the job he hired her for? Is this a good job for Danielle?

5. **Feeling Misunderstood**

And at an internship I had through my school, at a garden in a hospital, I also felt like being quiet made things harder for me. There was another intern there from a college who would walk around with a pad and pencil and jot down every word our boss said and ask a million questions about growing plants. I would just listen and later I would write down what I thought would be important for me to know in the future. My boss asked me, "Do you have any questions?" And I'd say, "No, I'm all right." But what I really wanted to say was, "The other intern already asked all I wanted to know. I don't think there's anything left to ask."

At the end of the internship, my boss told my teacher, "Oh, Danielle's a nice girl, but she's so quiet." I felt misunderstood.

6. **Maybe I Need to Speak Up?**

Then at my school my mentor, who I think is mad cool, told

31

**Q.** What impression do you think this made on her boss?

**Q.** Why does she feel angry and hurt? Why doesn't she change?

### REAL JOBS

me she was worried that I wouldn't do well on my final presentation because I'm quiet. I felt angry and hurt again. But the truth is, if everyone is saying I'm quiet, maybe it is a problem that I feel so unlike myself when I'm at school or on the job.

I have a card that I picked up from a bookstore when I was about 10 or 11 years old. It has pretty blue and pink clouds on it and on the top it says "Danielle" in big, bold letters. After that it reads, "God is your only judge." I still have that card to this day. I know people will always have something to say about me whether it's good or bad. And it hurts to hear them say that I'm quiet at school and work when I know that's not my true self. Ultimately, that card is right—what they say doesn't matter and only God can judge me. That card and my heart keep me grounded through all the criticism from bosses and teachers.

But I still hope that I can learn to feel more comfortable around authority figures. Maybe then they'll have a better idea of who the real me is, and it will be easier for me to be around them.

---

*Danielle was in high school when she wrote this story.*

32

# Explore the Ideas

## Discussion: Being Yourself (10 min)

Ask the Group:
- If Danielle wants to continue working in jobs like these, how would she need to change?
- What would she need to do to feel comfortable enough to stop being so "quiet"?
- Do you feel like you are a different person in different situations? What are some examples? How is it helpful? How is it a problem?

## Activity 1: The "Real" You
### Mingle, Mingle, Huddle, discussion (15 min)

This is a four-part activity. Tell participants that you are going to play a new version of the game called "Mingle, Mingle, Huddle."

Explain the rules: You are going to say, "Mingle, Mingle!" When you do, they are to walk around the room saying hello and introducing themselves to one another *as they would at school or on the street.* When they hear you say, "Huddle," they should find a partner and discuss the question you read aloud. (There may be one group of three if you have an odd number).

Start the activity by saying "Mingle, Mingle." After they've walked for a few seconds, say "Huddle." Ask this question: "What are three words you would use to describe yourself? Why?" Give them a minute to come up with their three words, and then stop them.

Next, tell them they're going to do the same activity, but with these changes: Instead of being friends on the street, they are in a workplace and everyone is a professional colleague. As they mingle, they meet and greet each other as professionals, not as casual friends.

Say, "Mingle, Mingle," and give them a minute to walk around introducing themselves (play-ing their professional roles). [If teens are having a hard time making the transition, suggest that they shake hands as they meet each other and make good eye contact as they talk.]

Then stop them again by saying "Huddle." When the teens are in pairs, tell them that one of them is an "employer" and the other is a potential "employee" seeking a job. (For this round, the employer can be the shorter of the two.) Tell employers to ask the following question: "What are three words you would use to describe yourself? Why?"

After a few minutes, stop them, ask them to SWITCH roles, and give the new "employee" a chance to answer the same question.

Finally, stop the group and discuss the following questions:

- What was the difference in how you behaved when you were just being yourself versus when you were the "employer" or the "employee"? For example, did the three words you used to describe yourself change? How?
- When you were the employer or the employee, did you feel like you were being "fake"? Why or why not?
- Is it important to always be "real"? Why or why not? What does it mean to be "real"?
- Can someone be "real" and professional at the same time?

## Activity 2: Your Best Qualities
### worksheet, pair share (10 min)

Ask participants to go to workbook p. 6 and complete the worksheet "Your Best Qualities" [Leader's Guide p. 49]. When everyone is finished, give participants an opportunity to share what they wrote with a partner.

## Activity 3: Portrait of a Professional
**writing and drawing, group share** (20 min)

Break participants into small groups and give each group a sheet of chart paper and some markers.

Then tell them they are to create a bubble (outline) picture of a "professional" person. The charts should look like the one on this page.

*Inside the lines*, they can write words or draw images to represent the things that make a person professional. *Outside the lines* they should write words or draw images to represent things that are "unprofessional." Give the groups about 15 minutes to work.

When the groups are done, give each group a chance to present their work to the larger group. Ask students to look at the words and images that each group has included inside and outside of the lines. Which ones stand out for them? Are there any surprises? Are there any words or images that they would move, or that could go both inside and outside? Why?

**Break** (15 min)

## Part I
## Activity 4: Communicating Professionally
**brainstorming, charting** (15 min)

Briefly describe *verbal* versus *nonverbal* communication. Then, on chart paper, brainstorm examples of each. (Examples of verbal communication might include whispering, talking, giving a speech, or yelling. Examples of nonverbal communication might include pointing, slouching, smiling, or sucking your teeth.) Mention that people will assess both their verbal and nonverbal communication to determine how professional they are.

Brainstorm and chart situations where participants will have to communicate with people at work, such as coworkers, bosses, and customers. For example:
• a coworker wants to switch shifts with you so he can go out Saturday night
• an employee wants to ask her boss for a raise
• several children need help at the same time and you're the only one on duty.

→Set the list aside. You will use it in Part II, below.

## Activity 5: Communication Styles Meet and Greet
**role play, brainstorm, discussion** (25 min)

*Note: Before the activity, copy and cut out the Communication Styles cards [Leader's Guide p. 50].*

Tell participants that you're going to discuss three different styles of communication: passive, aggressive, and assertive. Write definitions of each style on a flip chart.

**Passive:** doesn't take action or initiative, may come across as meek or shy
**Aggressive:** overly forceful and bold, may come across as bossy or controlling
**Assertive:** confident and direct, but values and respects others' feelings and opinions

Give each participant a "Communication Styles" card that says either "passive," "aggressive," or "assertive." Ask participants not to reveal what's on their card.

Ask participants to get up and act out their communication style using *nonverbal communication (body language) only*. The goal is to group themselves by the category on their paper. They cannot speak, write, or show their paper to others. When the groups are formed, ask participants to reveal their styles. Did they end up in the correct group? How were they able to figure out which group they belonged with?

Have participants stay in their "passive," "aggressive," or "assertive" groups, and ask them to brainstorm examples of how someone in this category might communicate. Give each group a sheet of chart paper and ask them to write examples of the following:
• verbal communication (things they might say)
• nonverbal communication (behaviors)
• pros and cons of this communication style
• advice for someone with this style on how they could communicate more effectively.

Have each team share with the larger group. Lead a discussion of how these different communication styles might play out in a work setting. Ask participants which category Danielle falls into. Which is the "best"? The "worst"? Why? Keep in mind that the "assertive" style is the one that is generally most positive, but it is important for young people to consider the value of the other two styles. For example, could they imagine how a football coach might use aggressive and assertive approaches, depending on the player or the situation? Or might a passive response sometimes be the best response in the moment to someone who is angry and irrational?

## Part II
### Activity 6: Communicating Professionally
**role play** (30 min)

Group participants in new groups of four or five. Assign each group one of the "communication situations" from Part I. Tell each group to create a role play of the situation. One person in each group should portray one of the three communication styles from the previous activity

(passive, aggressive, or assertive). The audience will have to figure out which communication style was portrayed.

Give each group a chance to perform their skit. Ask the audience which style they saw represented in the skit and how they knew. What did the character in the skit do that was effective? What could they have done differently? If the performance was of a passive or aggressive person, ask the group how an assertive person would have handled the same situation.

*Tip: If you are running short on time, you can ask for volunteers or randomly pick groups to perform instead of having everyone do it.*

### Activity 7: Time Is Money
**worksheet, pair share, brainstorming** (15 min)

Transition into this activity by pointing out that managing your time well (like being on time or finishing tasks by the deadline) is another big part of what it means to be professional.

Ask the teens if they've heard the expression "time is money." What do they think it means? Is it true? Why or why not? Ask why it's important to manage time well in general, and at work specifically.

Ask each student to complete the Time Management worksheet on p. 7 [Leader's Guide p. 51], which will take about five minutes. Then ask participants to find a partner and share their responses.

After they've had a chance to share, do a large group brainstorm. Ask the teens what tips and tools they have discovered for time management. (For example, does anyone lay out the clothes they will need for the next day the night before? Does anyone always try to arrive 10 minutes early to appointments? Get the group to share any time management strategies they already use. If they do not mention them, you should review the following three tools. Ask whether they use them, and why or why not.

*Planners:* You can buy daily, weekly, or monthly planners. Some people prefer to see just one day's worth of tasks at a time, while others need to see the whole month laid out for them. Some people prefer paper planners, and others use electronic ones.

*Alarm clocks:* Place your alarm clock far away from your bed so that you have to get out of bed to turn it off. Set more than one alarm to wake you up if you need to, especially for important events or on days when you have to wake up earlier than normal.

*To do lists:* Try to schedule similar tasks in "blocks" of time. For instance, if you have several errands to run in your neighborhood, plan to do them all at one time, rather then spreading them throughout the week.

Explain that being on time doesn't happen by accident, which is why we need to rely on these kinds of tools, and that we each need to find methods that work for us.

## Closing Activity (5 min)

Ask each participant to complete this sentence: **"One way I plan to be more professional is…"**

# Your Best Qualities

Take a moment and write as many of your positive qualities as you can think of. Try to come up with at least 10.

_____  _____

_____  _____

_____  _____

_____  _____

_____  _____

*When you finish, read through your list and CIRCLE the ones you think will help you be successful <u>at work</u>.*

Write one reason why you think one of those skills will be helpful to you.

_____

What is one thing about yourself that you might want to change when you're at work to help you be more successful?

_____

_____

How could you go about making that change? What is the first step you need to take to make that change?

_____

_____

**PASSIVE**

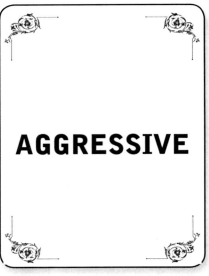

**AGGRESSIVE**

**ASSERTIVE**

**PASSIVE**

**AGGRESSIVE**

**ASSERTIVE**

**PASSIVE**

**AGGRESSIVE**

**ASSERTIVE**

# Time Management

Good time management is an essential skill in your personal life, at school, and at work. Take a few minutes to reflect on your own time-management skills as you answer the following questions.

1. Are you usually early, late, or on time? Why?

_____

_____

2. When do you usually do your homework?

☐ on a regular schedule     ☐ right before it's due     ☐ after it's due     ☐ never

3. How do you stay organized? What tools or strategies do you currently use to manage your time?

_____

_____

4. What makes it difficult to manage your time effectively?

_____

_____

5. List the most important things you have to do during the following parts of the day.

Before leaving the house in the morning: _____

During the workday: _____

Before leaving my job for the day: _____

Before going to bed at night: _____

6. What are three things you will to do to manage your time more effectively in the future?

_____

_____

_____

# SESSION 3: MONEY

## How to Manage It

# A Designer Addiction

## Story & Workshop Summary

**Time:** 180 minutes (including one 15-minute break)

**Materials:** chart paper, markers, pens or pencils, blank paper, slips of paper with scenarios written on them for "Real World Big Wind Blows" activity, tape, cards for Pictionary®/Taboo® Remix activity

**Story:** A Designer Addiction

**Core Emotions:** desire (status, attention), denial, self-control, determination to change

**Theme:** Spending all of your money on things to raise your status won't help you reach your goals in life. It could even prevent you from reaching them.

**Plot:** Delia is a recovering junkie. A pusher by the name of Ralph Lauren got her to join his posse when she was young, and soon other major designers were picking her pockets too. Unlike many of her friends, she was able to break the addiction "cold turkey."

**Youth Development Goals:**
• Young people will develop greater self-awareness of their beliefs and values about money.
• Young people will increase their knowledge of key terms related to money management.
• Young people will learn how to prepare a budget.

**Note:** *It is a good idea to review group guidelines at the beginning of each session.*

## Opening Icebreaker

**Sing It** (20 min)

Create groups of 3-5 people. Explain to the groups that they are going to play a competitive game. The goal of the game is to think of as many songs as possible that contain words related to the theme of money (in the lyrics or title). Distribute paper and pens so groups can list their songs.

The group that comes up with the most songs wins. The only rule of the game is that the songs have to be real songs. If another group challenges a song for any reason, the group presenting that song has to sing a bit of it to prove it's real.

*Tip: Consider limiting the number of challenges to three per team so the groups don't go overboard.*

Debrief:
• What values do these songs convey about money?

*Tip: There will be several messages depending on the songs. Help the teens identify messages that would be helpful to them in managing money and ones that would not be helpful.*

## Activity: Money Matters
**freewrite** (15 min)

Tell participants they're going to do a brief freewrite on money. Tell participants you will read three prompts. They will get 90 seconds to respond to each one.

To me, money means: _____

One of my concerns about money is: _____

One of my goals related to money is: _____

Debrief:
- Ask participants to turn to a partner and share one thing they wrote, if they are comfortable doing that. Then give participants the opportunity to share their response(s) with the large group. (No one has to share if they don't want to.)

Ask the group:
- Why does money matter?
- At what age should you learn how to manage your money? Why?

# Read the Story and Talk About It (20 min)

**Introduce the story:** Tell the class that you are going to read a story about a girl whose behavior seems to be limiting her potential to succeed in a job.

Take turns reading the story. Pause from time to time when there is a passage that you think is ripe for discussion. Ask the suggested questions, or add ones that you think will be helpful to your group.

Rudà Tillett

# A Designer Addiction

**By Delia Cleveland**

1. My name is Dee, and I am a recovering junkie. I was hooked on the strong stuff. Ralph Lauren wore my pockets thin. Calvin Klein was no friend of mine. And then guess what—I finally got the monkey off my back, although it took me a while to get on the right track.

   I got hooked on brand names six years ago when a Polo pusher by the name of Ralph got me to join his posse. It was easy. I had a part-time job and wasn't making much, but I didn't care. I scraped my last dollar to be able to wear Ralph's emblem on my chest like a badge of honor and respect.

   My mother told me I was messing up. Homework didn't matter anymore. Old friends were out. I was too fly to hang

*Note: Some (brand) names and prices have been updated in this story.*

47

**Q.** Why do you think she considered these brand label clothes to be a "badge of honor"? Do people respect you more when you wear designer labels? Should they?

## REAL JOBS

with them. Ralph offered me clout. The fellows adored me; the females were jealous. I became a fiend for the attention.

2. **Dollars Down the Drain**

It was all about me and Ralph L. until along came Calvin K., Tommy H., and this new guy named M. Ecko. We exchanged goods: my money for their names.

My mom started nagging me again. Out of worry she started snooping around my bedroom to see where my paycheck was going. She had set up a savings account for me, and I withdrew all the money—$1,000—to satisfy my habit. Then I charged $800 to my credit card for a quick fashion fix. Things were getting out of hand.

I didn't think I had a problem until the day my mother found the receipt in a shopping bag. She yelled that I was crazy. She wanted to know why I was giving all of my money to men who already had plenty. I told her she was behind the times and didn't know any better. I was looking good, and that's all that mattered . . .

. . . Until my money started getting tight. I was so busy buying more stuff that I couldn't do anything else. I even resorted to borrowing money from my mother. The more I took from her, the more she rubbed it in—I was sick. I needed help.

3. **Money for Clothes, But Not for the Train!**

Just to prove my mother wrong, I sought help. I wanted to show her that I could stop brand names from running my life, any time I wanted. It was my choice.

So, I chose to watch how other brand name users lived to see where they were headed. The big shock was, they weren't going anywhere. For example, one guy dipped in Mark Ecko was trying to talk to me in the train station. When the train came in, he asked me if there were any cops on the platform. I shrugged my shoulders and he hopped the turnstile. The guy

48

**Q.** What was she missing out on because she was spending all of her money on clothes? Do you think it was a good idea for her mom to lend her money? What should her mom have done about this situation instead?

**Q.** Do you think she has a real "addiction"? Can people actually get addicted to spending money or shopping? What might the consequences of that be?

had on $100 jeans and couldn't spare money for a train fare?

A popular jock at my school named Timmy (not his real name) used to boost Ralph Lauren clothing every single weekend. Even after getting locked up once, he continued to boost. I got bold and asked him his purpose. "I am taking from the White Man," he answered with a sly grin. "I'm going to keep geeing until I get caught again."

4. **Who's Getting Rich Here?**

"Get caught?" I wanted to say. "Get handcuffed for a white man?" But I kept quiet, because he—like me—didn't know any better. We were both addicted to the clothes. Timmy couldn't understand that while he was doing jail time for boosting, Ralph Lauren would still be collecting cars, furniture, and houses. Would Timmy care that while he was earning zero dollars a year looking good, Ralph Lauren would be worth millions?

Armed with this new knowledge, I vowed to leave brand names alone. I kept the clothes I had and started buying sensible clothes that looked fly. There was plenty to choose from. On the road to recovery, I bought $30 Levi's instead of $100 designer jeans. As a reward, I used some of the money I saved to treat myself to a Broadway play or a funky art museum. That made the withdrawal period less painful. My bank account got fatter and I got stronger.

When my friends started getting heavy into brand names, I tried to warn them. But they thought I was jealous and couldn't afford the stuff anymore. I explained that it was my choice not to support the luxury lifestyles of brand names dealers. They told me to mind my business; they could afford

**Q.** Is this true? Did she really "not know better"

**I scraped my last dollar to be able to wear Ralph's emblem on my chest.**

49

59

to wear what they wanted to wear.

**Q.** Is it her responsibility to "get through" to her friends? Why or why not? What do you think she could do to get through to them?

5. **I Could Only Save Myself**

I knew they couldn't afford to become dependent on brand names, but I couldn't get through to them. To this day, I see teenagers denying their addiction to brand names, even when the warning signs are obvious. If you or someone you love is going on four-hour bus trips to outlet centers just to get brand names; if you're selling drugs, stealing, or spending hard-earned money that you could use for college just to get brand names, get help.

> **On the road to recovery, I bought $30 Levi's instead of $100 designer jeans.**

Brand names is a powerful addiction that has destroyed many young lives. I was lucky. One outrageous receipt and an angry mother saved me from a life of make-believe self-importance.

From now on, my money is going to stay in my name. A nickel bag—$500—remains in my checking account. My savings account grows fatter with interest. I entertain myself with the finer things in life. I no longer look the part because I'm too busy living it. Calvin Klein was never a friend of mine. By the way, have you met him yet?

---

*Delia was 18 when she wrote this story.*
*She majored in creative writing at New York University*
*and later published two novels.*

50

# Explore the Ideas

### Discussion: Money Matters (10 min)

Ask:

• What does Delia mean when she says she no longer "looks the part" because she's too busy "living it"?

• How was she able to change her outlook on money so drastically? What did she lose by making this change? What did she gain?

### Activity 1: Gotta Have It, or Else!
**brainstorm, share out** (15 min)

Break participants into small groups and ask them to list the top five things teens "must have," in their group's opinion, in order to feel accepted by their peers. Ask them to order their list from the least to most expensive items.

Ask each group to share its list and discuss *where* the pressure to buy these items comes from. Do they really need all of these items? Why or why not?

### Activity 2: Real World Big Wind Blows
**musical chairs, discussion** (20 min)

*Note: Copy and cut out the Real World Big Wind Blows money cards in advance [Leader's Guide p. 64].*

#### Set up

— Arrange the chairs in a circle so there is one less chair than the number of participants.

— Tape one money card to the back of each chair.

— Have the teens stand in the center so they can't see the cards on the back of the chairs while you explain the rest of the game.

— Ask one participant to volunteer to go first. She will stand in the center of the circle. Everyone else should sit down in one chair without looking at the paper on the back.

— Give everyone a blank piece of paper and a pencil. Tell them that this piece of paper is their first imaginary paycheck for $300 from their job. Instruct everyone to write "$300" at the top of the page. Explain that they're going to play a game where they'll be earning and spending money.

#### Explain the rules

To start, everyone has a chair except for the person in the center of the circle. The game begins when the person in the center says, "The Big Wind Blows for anyone who…" and completes the statement with something true about him or herself, such as, "has brown eyes."

All of the people who have brown eyes, including the person in the center, must stand up and move to another chair that is empty. (Their new chair cannot be one that is right next to their starting chair.) The person left standing in the center now has to make another statement that is true about him or herself and several other people in the group. The process repeats.

## Not Enough Room?

If you are in a space where you do not have room to move around, you can do this activity in a different way. Give each participant a money card folded so they cannot see what it says. Tell them not to unfold it. Ask them to find a partner and exchange money cards. At that point, they should unfold the money card, add or subtract the appropriate amount of money from their $300 paycheck, refold the card, and then walk around the room until you tell them to stop again and find a new partner to exchange with.

Each time the participants get to their new seats, they have to read the scenario on the money card on the back of the chair and add or subtract the corresponding amount of money from their $300 "paycheck." (Before you begin, acknowledge that the arithmetic required in this activity may be hard for some people to do. Encourage participants to help each other out if they get stuck and to remain supportive and respectful of one another. You may gently use this as a teachable moment about the importance of basic math skills in most jobs.)

Play the game for a few rounds, and then start a discussion by asking the participants:
• How much money (if any) did you have left when the game was over?
• How much money went to things you needed versus things you wanted?
• Should we always think about saving some of our paycheck?

Debrief:
• Did participants have any control over their "spending" in this game? (Of course they didn't.) How is that different from real life? Facilitate a brief discussion on the idea that in real life we have a great deal of control over what we spend—if we choose to exercise it.

## Break (15 min)

## Activity 3: Financial Literacy Pictionary®/Taboo® Remix
### games (40 min)

Note: Copy and cut out the Pictionary®/Taboo® cards before the activity [Leader's Guide p. 67-68].

Break participants into small groups. Ask each group to quickly come up with a team name. Hand each group a few pieces of scrap paper (for drawing on) and a pen or pencil. Tell them that they are going to play a competitive game based on the games Pictionary® and Taboo®. Ask if anyone knows the rules of Pictionary® or Taboo®. If so, have them explain the rules to the group. If not, you will have to explain them.

Tell them that in Pictionary®, one person gets a secret word (that they don't show to the rest of the group). Their group has to guess the word based on what they draw. They cannot include any words in their drawing.

In Taboo, one person also gets a secret word (that they don't show to the rest of the group). Instead of drawing they *talk* to their teammates to try to get them to guess the word. The only rule is that they can't use any of the other words on the card, or any form of the word. So, if the secret word is "horse" and you can't say mane, or hoof, or Kentucky Derby, then you must give your clues without saying those words, or a word that includes horse, like horsepower.

Pick up the cards with financial literacy terms printed on them. Some of the terms will have to be illustrated on scrap paper (Pictionary®), and some explained without using certain prohibited words (Taboo®).

Shuffle the cards. Pick a group to go first, and ask one volunteer to pick a card. The volunteer must do what the card asks him or her to do—either draw (if the volunteer has a Pictionary® card, or talk (if the volunteer has a Taboo® card). The team has exactly one minute to figure out what term the volunteer is drawing or explaining.

*Tip: If the participant does not know what a term means, whisper it to them.*

If the team figures out the term, they get a point. The process is repeated with the other teams until the cards run out.

If a team gets the term wrong, the other teams will have 10 seconds to guess the term. If another team guesses correctly, that team earns a point. Remember to go over each term as it's guessed so everyone understands it. The definitions are in the Leader's Guide (p. 65] and in the student workbook [pp. 8-9].

Debrief:
- What new terms, if any, did you learn?
- Which terms are you still confused about?
- Is it important to know what these terms mean? Why?

*Note: Tell the teens that in addition to the definitions in the workbook (pp. 8-9), there are also brief descriptions of how people get suckered by banks, credit card companies, and other financial institutions. Encourage them to read those so they can make good decisions and avoid getting ripped off.*

### Activity 4: Budgeting for Success worksheet (20 min)

Ask students to complete the worksheet on p. 11, "Budgeting for Success" [Leader's Guide p. 70]. They can work either individually or in pairs. Ask participants to draw up a personal budget so that they are spending less than they are earning.

Give participants 10 minutes to complete their budgets. Then ask for volunteers to present their budgets to the large group.

Allow participants to respectfully critique each other's budgets by asking what was good about each and what they would spend or save differently. (There are no right or wrong answers. The goal is to get the group to see that people have different goals and different ways of thinking about money.)

Ask the group how much they set aside for savings in their budget and why. Mention that some adults aim to save a certain portion of what

they earn (e.g., 15%), to create an emergency fund. But for young people, it's easier to save if you set goals and then save toward them.

For example, teens could set a goal of saving enough this summer to pay for all college books next year (e.g., $800). Or they could save for something like an iPod. Or they could have a longer-term goal (e.g., "Save $5,000 by high school graduation so that I can move out and live on my own").

Explain that there are more than enough things to spend all of our money on every day: gadgets, lunch, movies, and more. Without a goal and a plan, most of us will just spend all the money we get. But people with goals—and especially teens who are being supported by their parents—can often save 50% or even 90% of their income.

## Closing Activity (5 min)

Ask each participant to complete this sentence: **"One way that I plan to be smarter about my money is…"**

Paycheck
+ $200

Bought sneakers
- $125

Visit to doctor
- $30
(co-pay)

Bought gift card
for sister's
birthday
- $30

Night out at
dinner and
a movie
- $30

Contribution to
help with rent
- $75

Earned money
for babysitting
+ $25

Took a
dance class
- $20

Bought new
jacket on sale
- $50

Bought a book
- $10

Bought the
latest cell phone
- $350

Received birthday
money from aunt
+ $50

# Financial Terms for Pictionary®/Taboo® Remix Activity

**Credit Card:** Credit cards allow you to buy something even if you don't have the money in your pocket.

*Credit card alert:* Unless you have the money in your bank account and can pay your bill in full at the end of the month, a credit card is a terrible way to buy things.

First, you pay interest on any balance you don't pay off at the end of the month. So, the $100 item you bought with a credit card may cost you an additional $20 in interest.

Second, there is very little time between when you get your credit card bill and when it is due. If you are late, you are charged a fee, which can be as high as $50. If you buy a $100 item, pay $20 in interest, and rack up two $50 late fees during the course of the year, you've just paid $220 for that $100 item.

**Bill:** A summary of charges for products or services. You get bills for cell phones, credit cards, utilities, etc.

*Bill alert:* Companies can make mistakes on bills—usually in their favor. You must carefully review every line of every bill you get before paying it. If you think there is a mistake, be prepared to spend a lot of time on the phone clearing it up.

**ATM:** These are the machines at the bank that allow you to make a withdrawal from your account or transfer funds between accounts, even when the bank is closed.

*ATM alert:* Don't become an ATM addict. If you're constantly taking out money and draining your account to zero, maybe you should just keep it under your bed. If you use a machine that is not from your bank, you will be charged. (It's a waste of your hard-earned money to pay $3 to take out $20, so it's important to choose a bank that has convenient and free ATM services.)

**Checking Account:** A bank account in which checks can be written against the amount deposited in the account. Checks, like credit cards, are handy ways to spend money when you don't have cash in your pocket.

*Checking account alert:* Like they have with credit cards, banks have set up checking accounts to make money from fees every time you make a mistake.

Here's how the bank can drain your checking account: Let's say you write a check and forget to deposit enough money to cover it. Your check "bounces" (it doesn't get paid). The bank will charge you a fee, say $25, for bouncing the check. The company you wrote it to may also charge a fee. So, if you write a $100 check to buy a jacket and bounce the check, you could easily end up paying $150 for that jacket.

**Bank:** Banks are a safer place to keep your money than your sock drawer. Having the money "out of sight" may make it less likely that you spend it. And many bank accounts pay interest, which means your money grows.

*Bank alert:* Most banks now charge fees for keeping an account, writing checks, and other services unless you keep an amount called a "minimum balance" in your account. Be sure you know what that balance is and what the fees are. If possible, don't open an account until you can get above the minimum balance and keep it there. Otherwise, those fees can eat away at your money.

**Check Cashing Place:** A business that will exchange a check for cash with no waiting period. These businesses charge a fee. For example, if the fee is 2% and you cash a $100 check, you only get $98 back. They can be more convenient for cashing checks.

*Check cashing alert:* In some states the fees are strictly regulated, so cashing checks there is relatively cheap. In other states, they can charge big fees, so you should try to cash your checks at the bank.

**Budget:** A plan for spending and saving money based on a person's goals during a given time period.

*Budget alert:* If you don't have a budget, your money may control you instead of vice versa.

**Savings Account:** A bank account that pays interest. Unlike checking accounts, some types of savings accounts

# Financial Terms for Pictionary®/Taboo® Remix Activity

do not allow you to withdraw money at an ATM. See "bank alert" for possible problems.

**Social Security:** A government program that provides financial assistance to people, starting at age 62 1/2. Social Security also provides benefits to people who are disabled, and "survivor benefits" to families where a parent has died. The Social Security tax that is deducted from your paycheck is used to fund this program. It's often called FICA on your paycheck stub.

*Social Security alert:* The amount of Social Security you receive is based, to some extent, on the amount you pay into the system and how many years you pay in. If you work off the books and do not declare your income at tax time, you may lose out on Social Security benefits. (Note: You are also not eligible for unemployment benefits if you work off the books.)

**Health Insurance:** A policy that pays specified amounts of money for medical expenses or treatments. Some employers pay for their employees' health insurance as a benefit of working for that company. Other employers offer health insurance, but require you to pay a portion of it. For example, you may have $50 a week deducted from your paycheck to cover your portion

of health insurance costs.

**Taxes:** Fees placed on income, property, or goods to support government programs, like summer youth jobs programs and schools. When you work, taxes are deducted from your paycheck.

**Stocks:** An investment that represents ownership in a company or corporation. Stocks are sold in units called "shares."

**Loans and Interest on Loans:** An arrangement in which a lender gives money to a borrower, and the borrower agrees to return the money by a certain time, usually with interest. For example, if you borrow $500 for one year to buy textbooks at 10% interest, you have to pay back $550.

*Loan alerts*—Good loans, not-so-good loans, and terrible loans: The best reason to borrow money is to pay for something that will be worth more in the future. For example, if you borrow a reasonable amount of money to go to college, and you graduate, you should earn enough to pay it back.

A not-so-good loan is for something nonessential that is guaranteed to decrease in value, like a bedroom set. If you're borrowing money for luxuries (instead of buying used), you may dig yourself into debt. Save up and pay cash for these items.

There are four especially terrible kinds of loans for young people. They often have high interest rates and penalties that really add up.

*Credit card loans:* Many people don't realize that if you don't pay off your credit card bill in full each month, the balance is a loan. And credit card companies often charge outrageous interest on that loan.

*Payday loans:* (where you borrow money and then pay it back when you get your next paycheck): These also tend to have very high interest rates, which eat away at your paycheck. If you wouldn't take a job that pays $3 an hour, you shouldn't take a payday loan either.

*"Rent-to-own" loans:* (where you get furniture, but you're really getting a loan): If you don't mind paying $600 for a $400 TV, then rent-to-own is perfect for you. If you don't like being suckered, then save up and buy the TV for $400 in cash.

*Income tax refund loans:* (where the company that prepared your taxes "loans" you the amount of your refund before the government sends it to you): These also have high interest rates. The government will send your check in a few weeks in most cases. Why not wait and get the full check instead of giving a big cut to the tax preparer.

**Tuition:** Tuition is a fee that students pay to gain a higher education. This fee pays for such things as instructors and facilities.

**TABOO®!**

YOUR GOAL IS TO GET YOUR TEAM-
MATES TO GUESS THE WORD IN
BOLD WITHOUT SAYING
ANY PART OF THE WORD
OR ANY OF THE WORDS BELOW IT.

### BUDGET
MONEY
PLAN
AMOUNT
SPEND

**TABOO®!**

YOUR GOAL IS TO GET YOUR TEAM-
MATES TO GUESS THE WORD IN
BOLD WITHOUT SAYING
ANY PART OF THE WORD
OR ANY OF THE WORDS BELOW IT.

### SAVINGS ACCOUNT
CASH
BANK
DEBIT CARD
CREDIT CARD

**TABOO®!**

YOUR GOAL IS TO GET YOUR TEAM-
MATES TO GUESS THE WORD IN
BOLD WITHOUT SAYING
ANY PART OF THE WORD
OR ANY OF THE WORDS BELOW IT.

### CHECKING ACCOUNT
CHECKBOOK
BANK
CASH
DEBIT CARD

**TABOO®!**

YOUR GOAL IS TO GET YOUR TEAM-
MATES TO GUESS THE WORD IN
BOLD WITHOUT SAYING
ANY PART OF THE WORD
OR ANY OF THE WORDS BELOW IT.

### SOCIAL SECURITY
BENEFIT
TAX
FICA
PAYCHECK

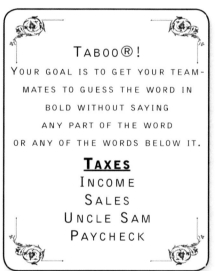

**TABOO®!**

YOUR GOAL IS TO GET YOUR TEAM-
MATES TO GUESS THE WORD IN
BOLD WITHOUT SAYING
ANY PART OF THE WORD
OR ANY OF THE WORDS BELOW IT.

### TAXES
INCOME
SALES
UNCLE SAM
PAYCHECK

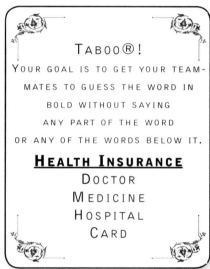

**TABOO®!**

YOUR GOAL IS TO GET YOUR TEAM-
MATES TO GUESS THE WORD IN
BOLD WITHOUT SAYING
ANY PART OF THE WORD
OR ANY OF THE WORDS BELOW IT.

### HEALTH INSURANCE
DOCTOR
MEDICINE
HOSPITAL
CARD

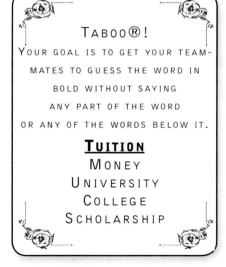

**TABOO®!**

YOUR GOAL IS TO GET YOUR TEAM-
MATES TO GUESS THE WORD IN
BOLD WITHOUT SAYING
ANY PART OF THE WORD
OR ANY OF THE WORDS BELOW IT.

### TUITION
MONEY
UNIVERSITY
COLLEGE
SCHOLARSHIP

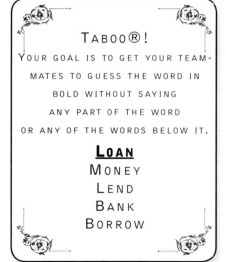

**TABOO®!**

YOUR GOAL IS TO GET YOUR TEAM-
MATES TO GUESS THE WORD IN
BOLD WITHOUT SAYING
ANY PART OF THE WORD
OR ANY OF THE WORDS BELOW IT.

### LOAN
MONEY
LEND
BANK
BORROW

**TABOO®!**

YOUR GOAL IS TO GET YOUR TEAM-
MATES TO GUESS THE WORD IN
BOLD WITHOUT SAYING
ANY PART OF THE WORD
OR ANY OF THE WORDS BELOW IT.

### STOCK
MARKET
SHARE
TRADE
BROKER

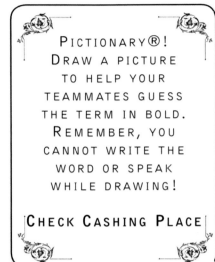

PICTIONARY®! DRAW A PICTURE TO HELP YOUR TEAMMATES GUESS THE TERM IN BOLD. REMEMBER, YOU CANNOT WRITE THE WORD OR SPEAK WHILE DRAWING!

**CHECK CASHING PLACE**

PICTIONARY®! DRAW A PICTURE TO HELP YOUR TEAMMATES GUESS THE TERM IN BOLD. REMEMBER, YOU CANNOT WRITE THE WORD OR SPEAK WHILE DRAWING!

**CREDIT CARD**

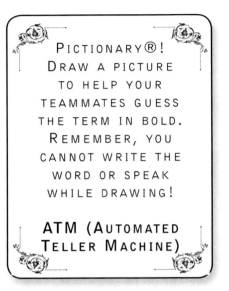

PICTIONARY®! DRAW A PICTURE TO HELP YOUR TEAMMATES GUESS THE TERM IN BOLD. REMEMBER, YOU CANNOT WRITE THE WORD OR SPEAK WHILE DRAWING!

**ATM (AUTOMATED TELLER MACHINE)**

PICTIONARY®! DRAW A PICTURE TO HELP YOUR TEAMMATES GUESS THE TERM IN BOLD. REMEMBER, YOU CANNOT WRITE THE WORD OR SPEAK WHILE DRAWING!

**BANK**

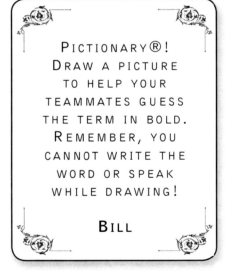

PICTIONARY®! DRAW A PICTURE TO HELP YOUR TEAMMATES GUESS THE TERM IN BOLD. REMEMBER, YOU CANNOT WRITE THE WORD OR SPEAK WHILE DRAWING!

**BILL**

# Sample Budget

Here's a sample budget with typical income and spending. Note that this persons budget includes $100 in savings. Use this budget to make your own budget on the next page with what you hope to earn, spend, and save.

Budget for the week of: July 9th - 15th

## *Income*

Work (after taxes): ............................................................... $190

Allowance/Other Income: ................................................... $40

**TOTAL INCOME:** $230

## *Amount I want to save:* $100

## *Mandatory Expenses:*

Transportation: ..................................................................... $20

Food: ....................................................................................... $25

Cell Phone Bill : ............................................................. $33

_____ : .............................................

## *Other Expenses:*

Movies with friends : ........................................................ $12

Other : .................................................................. $20

**TOTAL EXPENSES (including savings):** $210

**Any money left over? (income minus expenses):** $20

# Budgeting for Success

Based on the average amount of money you earn per week at your current job, create a budget below. Make sure you take into consideration all of the things you need to spend money on, as well as the things you want to spend money on and the amount of money you'd like to save for the future. Use the sample budget on the next page as a model if you get stuck.

Budget for the week of: _____

---

### Income

Work (after taxes): .................................................................... _____

Allowance/Other Income: ..................................................... _____

**TOTAL INCOME:** _____

---

### Amount I want to save: _____

### Mandatory Expenses:

Transportation: ................................................................................ _____

Food: ................................................................................................. _____

_____: ......................................................... _____

_____: ......................................................... _____

### Other Expenses:

_____: ......................................................... _____

_____: ......................................................... _____

**TOTAL EXPENSES (including savings):** _____

**Any money left over? (income minus expenses):** _____

# SESSION 4: HEALTH

## Manage Stress to Succeed

# Karate Killed the Monster Inside Me

## Story & Workshop Summary

**Time:** 180 minutes (including one 15-minute break)

**Materials:** chart paper, markers, pens, pennies (one per participant), "agree" and "disagree" signs

**Story:** Karate Killed the Monster Inside Me

**Core Emotions:** stress, anger, confidence

**Theme:** When we let anger or stress build up, it impacts us physically, mentally, and emotionally. Finding ways to manage strong emotions can have a positive effect on our health and our future success.

**Plot:** Robin is teased and bullied and finds himself feeling ready to "explode" from anger. At first he wants to learn karate to be able to fight his tormentors. But he discovers instead that karate actually teaches him how to control his emotions and avoid fighting.

## Youth Development Goals:

• Young people will understand that they can actively do things to control themselves and make themselves feel better.
• Young people will expand their repertoire of responses to stress.
• Young people will set personal goals for their own overall health and well-being.

**Note:** *It is a good idea to review group guidelines at the beginning of each session.*

## Opening Icebreaker

**Coin Flip** (10 min)
**step forward, step back**

Ask participants to stand in a line or lines toward one end of the room. They should have room to step backwards a few paces. Make sure there is enough space cleared for them to walk to the other end of the room.

Give each participant a penny. Tell them you are going to read them a story, and ask them to flip the coin when instructed and to follow the directions you give them.

### Story for Coin Flip Activity

It's 7:30 a.m. and you wake up to the sound of your alarm clock ringing. FLIP

*Heads: You went to bed early and got a good night's sleep. Take a step forward.*

*Tails: You stayed up until 4:00 a.m. chatting online with a friend and you're exhausted. Take one step back.*

You're getting ready to go to work at your job as a **summer camp counselor**, which you love. FLIP

*Heads: You decide to skip breakfast and get cranky and tired midmorning and snap at a colleague. Stay in your spot.*

*Tails: You make yourself a healthy breakfast and stay more alert and active all the way until lunch. Take a step forward.*

You leave the house and head to work. It's a beautiful summer day, not too hot and not a cloud in the sky. Your job is a 15-minute walk from your house, or a short bus ride. FLIP

*Heads: You decide walking would be good exercise. You arrive at work feeling invigorated and fresh.*

*Take two steps forward.*

*Tails: You don't feel like walking and decide to ride to work. Stay in your spot.*

You're on time for work and you feel ready to start your day. After several hours of doing arts and crafts projects with your campers, you realize it's time for lunch. One of the best parts of your job is that the staff refrigerator is always stocked full of food. You decide to head to the kitchen for your lunch break. FLIP

*Heads: You see some leftover nachos you can throw in the microwave and decide to eat them, along with a liter of soda. You grab a brownie for dessert. Take a step back.*

*Tails: You see some sandwiches that look healthy with whole wheat bread, turkey, and vegetables. You decide to have one, along with an apple and some water. Take a step forward.*

After lunch, you go back to work with the kids. One of them is giving you a really hard time and you're starting to feel stressed and frustrated. By the end of the day, you've completely had it and feel so stressed out you don't know what to do. Your supervisor, who you like and trust a lot, calls you into her office to see how you're doing. FLIP

*Heads: You discuss what happened with her and figure out a plan to handle things more effectively tomorrow. Take a step forward.*

*Tails: You tell your supervisor you're fine. Nothing gets resolved and you leave feeling tired and annoyed. Take a step back.*

On your way home from work, you run into someone you know from school. He's hanging out, smoking a cigarette. He says you look stressed and offers you one. FLIP

*Heads: You're still pretty stressed about work and decide to take the cigarette. Take two steps back.*

*Tails: You say, "No, thanks," head home, and take a relaxing bath instead. Take a step forward.*

When you arrive home there's a message from your Mom saying she'll be working late. Your best friend, who doesn't have a job, calls you and asks if you want to go out to a movie. FLIP

*Heads: You tell her you don't want to go out on a work night, but make plans for Friday. You heat up some leftovers, relax for a while, and go to bed early. Take a step forward.*

*Tails: You want to have some fun so you say yes, eat a large popcorn and soda instead of dinner, and don't get to sleep until midnight. Take a step back.*

Debrief:
• Why were some choices a step back? A step forward?
• What's hard about making healthy decisions?

## Discussion (brainstorm)
### Managing Stress (10 min)

Lead a large group brainstorm of what we think of when we hear the words "stress" and "health." Elicit that stress can be *caused* by unhealthy activities (like not getting enough sleep, or even drinking too much caffeine). Also elicit that stress can *contribute* to unhealthy activities, like snacking on junk food, even when you're not really hungry, or getting into fights. Stress is bad for our health, coming and going, so we need to find ways to manage it.

## Read the Story and Talk About It (20 min)

**Introduce the story:** Explain that you are going to read a story about a young man who makes choices that help him improve his own physical and mental well-being.

**Take turns reading the story:** Pause from time to time when there is a passage that you think is ripe for discussion. Ask the suggested questions, or add ones that you think will be helpful to your group.

Kenly Dillard

# Karate Killed the Monster Inside Me

**By Robin Chan**

1. I was fed up. From the time I was 4 years old, I was teased and pushed around by bullies on my way home from school because I was short and frail-looking. My family and I also got harassed by racist punks because we were the only Asian people living in a white neighborhood.

   These incidents grew the hate monster inside of me. Most days, I would come home from elementary school either angry or crying. My family and friends tried to comfort me, but I had been storing up the loads of anger inside me for too long. I thought I was going to explode.

**Q.** What can happen when you let anger or stress build up? How can it affect a person physically? Mentally?

82

74

*Learning the Culture*

2. **'My Hit List'**

When I was about 9, I found the answer to my problems. I decided to learn karate so I could break the faces of all the people on my "hit list" (anyone who had ever bullied me or my family).

I started nagging my parents about learning karate. They agreed because they wanted me to build up my self-esteem, learn some discipline, and have more self-confidence. All I wanted was to learn the quickest way to break someone's neck, but I didn't tell that to my parents.

I was about 10 years old when I finally got my chance. My first dojo (that's what martial arts students call the place where they study and practice) was small, musky, and smelled lightly of sweat. The instructor, Mr. Sloan, was as strict as an army drill sergeant.

Mr. Sloan taught us how to do strange abdominal exercises that were like upside down sit-ups and really difficult. He wouldn't allow any slacking off from people who got tired. It was only the first day—what did he want from us? I quickly discovered that I was really out of shape. Before the first lesson was over, I was already thinking about dropping out.

3. **Learning Skills and Getting in Shape**

By the end of the second lesson, however, I had decided to stick with it. Mr. Sloan was teaching us cool techniques for breaking out of arm and wrist locks and that got me interested.

Mr. Sloan was a good instructor. Within a few months, my class of beginners went from learning the basic punch, block, and kick, to learning a flying jump kick. He also taught us effective techniques for breaking out of headlocks and strangleholds. We enhanced our skills by sparring with each other and practicing at home.

Although the dojo had limited resources (there were no boards to break, no martial arts weapons, and no fighting gear), I still learned a lot and had a lot of fun. I became more flexible from the rigorous exercises. In addition to practicing our karate

83

## REAL JOBS

moves, we did push-ups, sit-ups, and leg, arm, torso, and back stretches to limber up.

4. **Killing Problems With Meditation**

We also meditated together. Near the end of class, Mr. Sloan would "guide" us through the meditation by telling us to clear our minds. One time, he told us to picture ourselves breaking free of a barrier or knocking a barrel or a wall to pieces. He said that whenever we had problems or faced challenges that got us frustrated, we should go to a quiet place, relax, and close our eyes. In our minds, we should picture ourselves knocking over that problem or challenge. Mr. Sloan said that doing this should make us feel better. After meditating on "killing" the problem, he said, our minds would be clear and we'd be more determined to solve it.

> **I had been storing up the loads of anger inside me for too long.**

5. **Learning Respect**

Mr. Sloan also made it clear that he was teaching us karate not just so we'd be able to kick someone's ass real good, but so each of us could become a role model. A role model, he explained, was someone with a good conscience, good morals, self-respect, and respect for others.

We worked on developing these qualities in class by bowing to the instructor, addressing him as "sir" or "sensai," treating fellow students with respect, and listening to our sensai's lectures, which taught us about respect, discipline, manners, and so on. We were taught to exercise these qualities not only in the dojo, but outside as well.

The goal of becoming a role model was a major factor in my wanting to continue to study karate. I no longer saw the martial arts as a way to get back at people who hurt me. I knew from

84

**Q.** What is meditation? Why would meditation be part of a karate class? Aren't they opposites? Or are they related somehow?

**Q.** Do you think this will work for Robin? Have you ever tried a technique like this to help you deal with stressful situations? What was it? Did it help?

*Learning the Culture*

experience that there were enough menacing and evil people in this world. I didn't want to become one of them.

6. **Discipline Helped Me Stay in Control**

After a few months, I was much more self-confident and disciplined. I knew that I was now capable of protecting myself against enemies. Whether or not I chose to fight someone who bullied me was beside the point; I knew that I could knock them out. Just knowing that made me feel good about myself, so why fight when you're already ahead? Besides, not fighting would save my knuckles from a lot of pain.

The insults and slurs I encountered did not bother me as much anymore. As a matter of fact, the discipline and basic philosophy I learned from karate held back the punches I was tempted to throw when people tried to provoke me to fight.

For example, one day when I was walking home from school, two teenaged guys walked into me. One of them said, "Watch it, ch-nk" and shoved me. They started pushing me but I just blocked their pathetic pushes. They weren't getting enough thrills from just shoving me, so they started cursing and spitting at me too.

7. **I Didn't Need to Fight**

I started getting really aggravated. Then I remembered something Mr. Sloan had told me when I asked him what to do when someone bothers you. "Low-lifes like these do not deserve the time and energy you put into punching them out," he said. "Just walk away and splash some cold water on your face."

I cooled down and started walking away. The two guys saw that I was not affected by their stupid remarks. I heard one of them say, "Forget that ch-nk, man."

It was ironic how I wanted to learn karate so that I could beat up people like these, and then, when I got the chance, I didn't go through with it. What karate taught me was that fighting isn't the right way to solve a problem. It just turns you into one of those

**Q.** Is it OK to walk away from a fight or argument or should you always defend yourself in some way? What's the benefit to Robin of walking away?

85

REAL JOBS

low-lifes who don't have the conscience, respect, manners, or education to know how to handle their problems any other way.

I was good enough at karate by that point that it wouldn't have been a fair fight. But if I had given in to the temptation to beat those guys up, I would have felt ashamed and guilty. I would have disappointed Mr. Sloan, who taught me that the most important rule of karate is not to fight unless it's necessary for self-defense; my parents, who told me never to fight with anyone even if they are wrong; and myself, because I feel that it is wrong to take advantage of a situation.

8. **Becoming a Role Model**

The time and effort I was putting into karate was getting me worthwhile results. I used to be wild when I was with my friends, but I had become more reserved and well-behaved. I also used to slack off in school but not anymore. I really started gearing up and hitting the books. My teachers and parents noticed the difference and were happy with what they saw.

**Q.** Have you ever tried to change a bad habit or behavior? What did you do that helped you change?

> What karate taught me was that fighting isn't the right way to solve a problem.

I was even becoming a role model for some of my friends. They told me that they had never seen me work so hard before, and they admired the high grades I was earning in school. They decided to follow my example and started pulling their acts together and improving their own grades.

Unfortunately, Mr. Sloan's class ran for only a year and when time was up, all of us were really upset. But our instructor had a new class of misfits to turn into the fine role models we had become.

Studying karate was a wonderful experience. I'm thankful to my extraordinary instructor, Mr. Sloan, and to my great fam-

**Q.** Why did his experience with karate have an impact on these other areas of Robin's life?

86

ily who let me go to the dojo and have supported me always. Together, Mr. Sloan and my parents have made me realize that I should always try my best and put a sincere effort into whatever I do. They have geared me up, morally and spiritually, to reach for the stars.

*Robin was 16 when he wrote this story.*
*After college and graduate school, he became*
*a flight surgeon for the U.S. Air Force.*

**Q.** How do you think his experience with karate will impact his future success? Will it help him? How?

## Explore the Ideas

### Discussion: Healthy Choices (10 min)

Ask the Group:
 • What do you think would have happened if Robin hadn't taken up karate?
 • What if he hadn't tried meditation?
 • What if he had gotten into that fight instead of walking away?

### Activity 1: Stop Stressin' Me
**brainstorm, charting** (10 min)

Ask the group, "What are some of the consequences of unchecked stress?" Get several suggestions.

Then ask the group to come up with all the ways they can think of that people deal with stress. Record these responses on chart paper.

Ask: "Which of the responses on the chart paper are healthy?" If students have a hard time identifying "healthy" responses, explain that a "healthy response" is one that moves you toward your goals, not away from them, and doesn't harm you or others. (For example, if you feel disrespected by your supervisor, it may feel better in the short term to curse her out, but that's not a healthy response because it harms your longer-term goal of being successful on the job.)

Circle the items on the chart paper that students consider to be healthy responses to stress. Ask, "Which of the healthy responses would be effective in the workplace?" (For example, an effective response to stress at home might be to take a nap, but it wouldn't work on the job.)

### Activity 2: How I Handle Stress
**social barometer** (25 min)

Tell the group that the previous activity explored how people in general respond to stress.

Now we are going to look at how we deal with stress.

Post a sign on one side of the room that says "agree" and a sign on the other that says "disagree." Ask participants to stand in the center of the room. Explain that you are going to read a series of six statements. For each statement you read, you will ask them to stand on the side of the room that corresponds to their reaction to each statement. Once everyone has taken their position in response to the statement—ask a few people in each location to explain their position. Participants may remain in the middle if they are neutral or unsure.

Read these statements. After each statement, discuss why people are standing at "agree" or "disagree":
 • It's easy for me to handle the stress at my job.
 • People should not bottle up their frustration, even at work.
 • I can usually control how stressed out I get.
 • How healthy I am depends mostly on the choices I make.
 • It's important for me to keep my cool even when someone insults me.
 • It would be stressful to talk with my supervisor about a problem I'm having at work.

### Activity 3: Releasing the Stress
**deep breathing, freewrite** (10 min)

Tell participants you're going to do a deep breathing relaxation exercise. During the exercise they should breathe very slowly—in through their nose and out through their mouth.

Ask participants to close their eyes and take a long, slow, deep breath—feeling their chest rise as they slowly fill their lungs with air, and then fall as they slowly exhale. Repeat three times. Speak slowly and calmly each time to create a sense of relaxed calmness in the room. Then ask them to open their eyes. Ask if they already feel a little calmer or relaxed. (Some will.)

Explain that this kind of breathing exercise is something you can do to help yourself calm down if you are stressed out or nervous.

Ask participants to complete a freewrite on the following prompt for 90 seconds:

*What does it feel like to be stressed out? How easily do you get stressed out or angry? What really stresses you out or makes you mad? How do you deal with your own stress?*

When time is up, ask participants to turn to a partner and share one thing they wrote. [Note: Tell them they are not allowed to share anything about anyone in the room who "stresses them out."] Then give participants the opportunity to share their response(s) with the large group, if they choose. (If no one mentions it, elicit that while it always good to avoid moodiness and angry outbursts, it is especially important to avoid it on the job. Don't yell at your supervisor or roll your eyes.)

**Break** (15 min)

## Activity 4: Managing Stress at Work
**worksheet, share out** (20 min)

Tell the group that the best way to equip yourself to handle stress is to maintain overall good health—mental and physical.

Give each student about 10 minutes to complete the worksheet "Managing Stress at Work" on p. 12 [Leader's Guide p. 83]. Then ask participants to form groups of three to discuss what they wrote. Give them a few minutes to talk in their small groups. Ask participants to share one thing they wrote with the large group.

Explain that a major cause of stress is having lots of responsibility but little control. The best way to reduce stress is to figure out ways to have more control in any given situation (or less responsibility). For instance, if you have a lot of tasks to complete at work but don't know how to complete them, you're likely to get very stressed. To deal with that, you could ask your supervisor to explain your responsibilities to you more clearly. If you have too much to do, you could ask a coworker to help you complete some of your work. (Remember that you can be there to help them out when they get stressed, as well.)

## Activity 5: Stress on the Job
**role play/skits** (45 min)

Ask participants for examples of stressful situations they might encounter at work. Record the responses on chart paper. Then break participants into groups of four or five.

Tell them they are going to choose one of the stressful situations on the list to depict in a role play. They should prepare TWO different skits.

1) Unhealthy: The first skit should show the main character reacting to the stressful situation in a *negative* or *unhealthy* way and the consequences of that response at work.

2) Healthy: The second skit should show the same situation, but this time with the main character reacting to the stressful situation in a more positive or healthy way. Give the groups up to 15 minutes to prepare and practice.

When time is up, ask each group to perform both versions of their skit. After each scene, ask the audience what they saw. Give participants a chance to offer constructive feedback about how well they think the healthy and positive responses would work in real life. Give them a chance to share examples of stressful situations they have faced on the job and their responses.

If there's time, and there is a relatively high level of trust in your group, consider giving participants a chance as a large group to "problem-solve" or give advice to any participants in the group who are facing stressful situations at work that they don't know how to handle.

## Closing Activity (5 min)

Ask each participant to complete this sentence: **"One thing I plan to do to help me deal with stress is..."**

# Managing Stress at Work

What does it feel like to be "stressed out"? What happens to your body? What happens emotionally?

What are some sources of stress at your job?

What are some ways that you currently deal with these stresses?

Which of these do you think are "healthy" and effective ways to deal with stress? Why?

What can you do when you're at work to avoid getting "stressed out"?

How could your colleagues help you avoid or manage your stress? What help do you want from them? What are you willing to accept?

# SESSION 5: COLLEGE

## You Can Do It. Here's How

# My First Semester
## Overworked, Underpaid, & Unprepared

## Story & Workshop Summary

**Time:** 180 minutes (including one 15-minute break)

**Materials:** chart paper, markers, pens, blank paper, tape, cards for "College Application Calendar" activity

**Story:** My First Semester—Overworked, Underpaid, & Unprepared

**Core Emotions:** excitement, disappointment, anxiety

**Theme:** It's important to find a good match between your interests and needs and the school you attend

**Plot:** Troy hopes to attend college far from home, live in a dorm, and have a supportive campus experience. But when he's rejected from his first-choice school, he finds himself at a school that doesn't fit his needs and makes him question if he's even cut out to attend college.

**Youth Development Goals:**
• Young people will increase their understanding of the value of higher education.
• Young people will increase their knowledge of the vocabulary related to higher education.
• Young people will identify the characteristics of the school that fits their personal and intellectual needs.
• Young people will map out the college application process.

*Note: It is a good idea to review group guidelines at the beginning of each session.*

 **Opening Icebreaker**

**Find Someone Who. . .** (15 min)

Ask each participant to open the workbook to p. 13, "Find Someone Who..." [Leader's Guide p. 95]. Explain that they will have to find someone for each item on the page and have that person sign his or her name. The first person to get all signatures for all of boxes/lines is the winner.

Give the group five minutes to find as many people as they can, then share some responses with the large group. Discuss the idea that people tend to assume that everyone knows all the college "jargon" (words used to convey special meaning), but that not everyone does. Today's workshop will be a chance to learn some things you might not know about college.

## Read the Story and Talk About It (20 min)

**Introduce the story:** Explain that you are going to read a story about one young man's experience applying to and attending college.

**Take turns reading the story:** Pause from time to time when there is a passage that you think is ripe for discussion. Ask the suggested questions, or add ones that you think will be helpful to your group.

Kingslee Gourrick

# My First Semester: Overworked, Underpaid, and Unprepared

### By Troy Shawn Welcome

1. When I was younger, I used to imagine what my life after high school would be like. I saw myself going away to a small, supportive college, living in a dormitory, meeting new people, and having new experiences. I never thought that I would have any difficulty merging onto the highway of adult life. Now almost a year has passed since I graduated from high school and I've found that making it in the world of responsibilities, bills, priorities, and decisions is harder than I thought.

When the time came to apply to college, I was sure of only one thing—I wanted to go away to school. I never wanted to attend school in New York City where I grew up because there are too many distractions here. I worried that I would be hang-

61

**Q.** What would be the advantages for Troy if he went away for college? What would be the advantages of staying local?

## REAL JOBS

ing out with my friends too much and not devoting enough time to studying. So I decided to apply to a few SUNY schools and to Sarah Lawrence College, a private school about 30 minutes from the city in Bronxville, New York. As a last resort, I also applied to some CUNY schools.*

I found out about Sarah Lawrence from the guidance counselor at my high school. He went to college there and told me that the school was famous for its writing program. Since I was what some people considered a born writer, he thought Sarah Lawrence would be perfect for me.

2. **The Perfect School for Me**

After I visited Sarah Lawrence's campus for a weekend I agreed that it was perfect for me. Most of the people were friendly and found time in their schedules to entertain me. I went to a party on campus, played pool with some other students, and saw a movie in the campus theater. I liked the atmosphere.

> **All the classes I was planning to take had been filled. What was I supposed to do now?**

While I was there, I also attended a couple of classes so I could get an idea of what the work was like. I went to a literature class on Saturday morning and most of the people there looked as if they had slept in the classroom, including the professor. It shows a lot when people are comfortable enough to go to class in what looks like their pajamas. I've always felt that small, comfortable classes served me better than large, impersonal ones. I left that Sunday with a love for Sarah Lawrence and the idea that I could spend the next four years there.

---

*SUNY and CUNY schools are public colleges in New York. SUNY is the State University of New York, and most of its schools are outside of New York City. CUNY is the City University of New York, and all of its schools are in New York City. Both systems include everything from community colleges to graduate schools.*

*Managing Your Time*

3. **Scrambling for a Second Choice**

Unfortunately, I wasn't accepted, and that's when my problems started. I wasn't particularly interested in going to any of the public SUNY colleges—I hadn't even completed the applications. I had thought I was a shoe-in for Sarah Lawrence. I had only considered SUNY in the first place because my counselor had told me that it's better to apply to a lot of schools so that I'd have some choices. I guess he was right.

Since I had completed my CUNY applications, I still had the option of going to a city school. I had heard many good things about Baruch from my counselor, so it became my first choice. Luckily, Baruch also chose me.

At first, I was excited to know that I'd be going to Baruch. Actually, I was excited to be going anywhere. It was extremely important to me to get a college education because I'd be only the second person in my family to attend college. (My brother was the first.) In all the excitement, I can't say that I really envisioned what the first day would be like, but I sure didn't expect what I saw at registration.

> **Q.** Why do you think Troy didn't apply to other schools like his counselor suggested?

4. **The First Day Was Hell**

When I walked into the registration building at Baruch, I experienced what I considered "college hell." There were people on lines, on stairs, in front and in back of me. They all looked confused and upset. I wondered what the problem was.

I had a 3 o'clock appointment, so I strolled over to the right line, secure in the knowledge that I already had my schedule planned out. I had attended a summer orientation where I was given the fall semester course catalogue and instructed on how to arrange my schedule.

I soon found out that none of that mattered. The guy circling the room wasn't handing out college leaflets; he was handing out lists of available courses. Every 15 minutes, he came around with a new list—it seemed that the longer I stood on line, the more courses got closed. Wait a minute! All the classes I was planning

63

REAL JOBS

to take had been filled. What was I supposed to do now?

My mind was scrambling for answers when I began to notice the two other packed lines that were ahead of the one I was on. Those people had appointments for 1:45 and 2:30. The majority of them were squatting on the floor—they had been waiting so long that their legs wore out. It was then that I got the courage to glance at my watch. It was already 4:30 and I was frustrated (my appointment was for 3:00 p.m., remember?). And I had to be at work by 6.

5. **I Needed a Paycheck**

I changed my schedule two more times while on line and then three more as I sat with the counselor. Then I walked toward the cashier to pay for the scraps I ended up with. I was given African studies, psychology, and the usual math and English courses.

By the time I was three weeks into the semester, I was already having to force myself to go to class. My African studies course was one of the straws that broke the camel's back. It was a lecture class, which should've been easy. We just had to read certain chapters in our textbook along with attending lectures.

Since I hardly had time to work full-time and read books, I tried to get as much as I could from the lectures. But the professor had a very thick accent and I needed an interpreter to understand 90% of what was being said. That's when I started falling behind.

My psychology class was better. Even though there were about 500 students, the two professors who taught it always added a dash of humor to their lectures, which made it fun. But the fact that it was the only class I had on Tuesday afternoons was a problem.

I was working nights (from 6:00 p.m. to 12:30 a.m.), and after sleeping most of the day I hated having to go downtown for a 3 o'clock class and then rush back uptown to get to work on time. I was putting more value on my paycheck than my education. I used to say that if school would pay me I would go more often.

64

**Q.** What is Troy's dilemma? Which do you think is more valuable, school or work? How can Troy solve his dilemma?

6. **It Didn't Feel Like College**

   The biggest problem was that I didn't feel like I was experiencing college life. Baruch didn't have dormitories, a large campus, or the feel of college. Most of the people there, myself included, just went in, went to class and then went to work. But that wasn't what I wanted.

   I wanted to live on a campus away from my usual environment. I wanted school to be my life for four years. I wanted to eat, sleep, and party in or around my campus. I wanted to feel connected to the other students. But most of the people who attend CUNY schools are too busy trying to support themselves while educating themselves to have time to experience each other.

   Since I wasn't getting what I wanted out of college, I quickly grew tired of working long and hard just to pay for books and that ridiculous tuition. To make a long story short, I ended up leaving school in the middle of my first semester, after only three months.

   It wasn't until I left school that I realized why I failed at one of the most crucial challenges of my life. I think I set myself up to fail because I never dreamed of going to school in the city. I had always imagined myself on a college campus away from everyone and everything I had grown accustomed to during the last 19 years of my life. So when I had to attend a city school, failing was my way of rebelling.

7. **Wasting My Life Away**

   I came to the conclusion that I wasn't ready for college, or maybe I was too lazy. After I left school, I continued working as a telephone interviewer with full-time hours. It wasn't a difficult job. All I had to do for eight hours a night was call people across the nation and type their answers to surveys into a computer. But I felt like my life was worthless.

   When I was in school I felt a little productive, but now all I did was work all night and sleep all day. I felt like I was wasting my pitiful life away. My job wasn't even stable—there wasn't

**Q.** What do you think he means by this? Who or what is he rebelling against?

65

**REAL JOBS**

always a lot of work, so I couldn't rely on my checks being the same amount every payday.

I finally quit, thinking I could find a better job and start to make a decent living for myself until I was ready to go back to school. Truthfully, I didn't really want another job, but I did want money to buy the things I needed and to support my social life. The problem was that most jobs asked for both a college degree and a lot of skills. Even though I had some skills, I didn't have a college education. It's too bad I couldn't get paid for watching talk shows every morning.

8. **Back On Track**

Talk shows can fill up your day, but I was bored and sinking deeper into depression. After a month or two of unemployment, I told myself that there was no way for me to have the things I want in life without college.

I realize now that I am cut out for college—just not the college I ended up at. Right now, I'm trying to get into a SUNY school. That way I'll be able to live on campus the way I always imagined I would. Now that I've experienced first-hand what it's like to live in one place, work in another place, and go to school someplace else, I'm more convinced than ever that I need to eat, sleep, and breathe college in order to succeed.

*Troy was 20 when he wrote this story. He went back to college and graduated from SUNY-Purchase, then got a master's degree in education administration and became a high school principal.*

**Q.** Do you think Troy is ready for college? Why or why not? If he gets accepted to an upstate school, what challenges do you think he will face?

66

# Explore the Ideas

## Discussion: Why Go to College?

Ask the Group:

**Why do people decide to go to college?**

Chart responses on a sheet of chart paper.

If the students don't mention them, elicit some of the things that were mentioned in the story, including the fact that many jobs now require a bachelor's degree, and that college graduates usually earn more money than those with only a high school diploma. Ask them to look at the Education Pays chart in their workbook, p. 21 [Leader's Guide p. 108]. What do they notice about how salaries change in these professions as people get higher degrees and certification?

## Activity 1: Finding a College that Fits
**brainstorm, worksheet, drawing** (35 min)

Do a brief brainstorm with the group: Ask them to shout out ideas about what it will be like to be in college.

Then, tell students that a key to college success is finding a good fit between their skills and interests and what the college has to offer. Ask participants to take 10 minutes to complete answers to the questions on the workbook p. 14 titled "Finding a College that Fits" [Leader's Guide p. 96]. When time is up, break participants into small groups. Ask them to take a few moments to share.

Next, give each group a piece of chart paper and markers. Ask students to work in groups to draw a "map" of the college or university they would like to attend, considering the information they just shared with each other. They may not be in total agreement on all of the points, but the map should represent at least one preference of each group member.

Give participants 20 minutes to draw their maps. When everyone is done, allow each group to present their work. Talk about the various things people take into consideration when choosing a college and why each is important. Ask: "Which of the factors you wrote down were the most important to you? Why?"

## Break (15 min)

## Activity 2: College Vocabulary
**group quiz** (20 min)

Tell the participants: To talk about college, we need to use and understand college vocabulary.

Break the participants into teams of four or five. Ask each group to open the workbook to the "College Vocabulary Quiz," p. 15 [Leader's Guide p. 97]. Tell them to work together for 10 minutes to complete the quiz as a group. When time is up, review the quiz with the entire group. Go over any confusing terms and answer any questions. (If you don't know the answer, that's fine. You're not expected to be a college expert.)

## Activity 3: College Application Calendar
**worksheet** (25 min)

*Note: In advance, copy and cut up enough sets of the 12 "College Calendar" cards so that each small group will have one set [Leader's Guide p. 100-103].*

Divide participants into groups of 3-6. They are going to work together to complete the activity on workbook p. 16, "College Application Calendar" [Leader's Guide p. 98]. Tell each group to create a college calendar on the board or using a few sheets of chart paper that has the five sections in the calendar in the workbook (Fall and Spring semester of junior year; Summer; and

Fall and Spring semester of senior year). When each group is ready, hand each group of set of "College Calendar" cards. Tell them that when you say, "Begin," they have to figure out which steps go in which months of the calendar. Give them 5-10 minutes. Walk around the room and ask questions to prompt them, if necessary.

When they're done, have groups present their calendars. Pay special attention to disagreements or events that are definitely out of order. Help them to get their steps in order. Explain to them that the college application process does have an order, and they need to follow it. If they haven't noticed, tell them that a correctly completed copy of the calendar is on p. 28 of their workbook for them to keep for future reference.

## Activity 4: You're the Admissions Officer! (30 min)

Break participants into groups of four or five. Explain that they are members of a college admissions committee (the people in charge of deciding who gets into the school and who does not). Assign each group one of the colleges on the list in the workbook, p. 17 [Leader's Guide p. 104]. Ask them to read the description of their college and then consider the applicants on p. 18 of the workbook [Leader's Guide p. 105]. They will work together to decide which of the applicants they will accept into their school. They should read the descriptions, decide as a group which candidates to accept for their school, and be able to explain their decisions. Give them 15 minutes to work on this. Then give each group a chance to explain their decisions.

As a large group, discuss:

• **Did the groups all choose the same candidates? Why or why not?**

• **What were the most important things you looked at when deciding?**

• **Do you think an actual admissions committee would make the same decision if they had to choose one of these candidates? Why or why not?**

• **What did you learn about college admissions from this activity?** (Elicit that there is is a college that is a "right fit" for every high school graduate who is serious about continuing to college.)

## Activity 5: Developing a Plan for Applying to College
worksheet (15 min)

Ask participants to go to the worksheet on p. 20, "My Plan for Applying to College" [Leader's Guide p. 107]. Give participants a few minutes to write their responses to the questions on the page. When they are done, ask for volunteers to share their responses.

## Closing Activity (5 min)

Ask each participant to complete this sentence: **"The next step I need to take to reach my education goal(s) is…"**

# Find Someone Who...

You will have about five minutes to get as many signatures as possible. Find a person who fits the description and ask them to sign their name. No one can sign your paper more than once.

Knows what FAFSA stands for: _____

Has visited a college campus: _____

Can name three colleges or universities in New York City: _____

Has taken the SAT or PSAT: _____

Knows what the common application is: _____

Has a friend or family member who is currently enrolled in college: _____

Will be the first in their family to attend college: _____

Knows what BA stands for: _____

Knows where they want to go to college: _____

Plans to earn a master's degree one day: _____

Can name at least two state (public) colleges in your state: _____

Can name at least two private colleges or universities in your area:

_____

# Finding a College that Fits

College is a big investment of money and time, so it's important to plan carefully when choosing a school. Respond to the following questions by imagining a school that's right for you:

**1. What kind of setting is the school in?**

☐ urban   ☐ suburban   ☐ rural

**2. What size school seems like it would be comfortable for you?**

☐ Tiny (under 2,000)   ☐ Small (2,000-5,000)
☐ Medium (5,000-10,000)
☐ Large (more than 10,000 students)
☐ Size doesn't matter

**3. Who attends your school? (Think about race, gender, where people come from, etc.)**

☐ Mostly people from my city or area
☐ Mostly people from outside my area
☐ Mostly well off people
☐ Mostly working- or middle-class people
☐ Mostly people of my race or background (e.g., black, Catholic, etc.)
☐ Mostly people different from me
☐ Mostly people who live on campus
☐ Mostly people who live at home or somewhere else

**4. How far is your school from home?**

☐ A bus or subway ride
☐ A car, Greyhound, or Amtrak ride
☐ A plane ride

**5. What does it physically look like?**

☐ Suburban or rural campus with dorms, lots of trees and grass. Almost all activities, including social activities, take place on campus, unless you have a car.

☐ Urban campus with office buildings.

☐ "Urban oasis." In a big city, but with a separate campus with grassy student areas.

**6. What majors should this school have? (e.g., English? business? computer science? nursing? etc.)**

_____

**7. How would you spend free time there? (Rank from 1-4 in order of importance.)**

_____ Studying        _____ Volunteering

_____ Working         _____ Other

**8. How large are most of the classes?**

☐ Seminars (6-12 students)
☐ Like HS classes (20-30)
☐ Large lectures (50-750)

**9. Where do you want to live?**

☐ At home   ☐ In an apartment
☐ In a dormitory
☐ In a sorority or fraternity house

**10. How much do you expect to spend to attend this school for tuition, room, and board?**

☐ $6,000-$12,000/yr (tuition and books at a CUNY or other local public college)

☐ $15,000-$25,000/yr (tuition, books, room, and board at a typical state school

☐ $35,000-$55,000/yr (tuition, books, room, and board at a private school)

(Note: Scholarships, loans, and jobs can cover some of these costs.)

**11. What other factors are important to consider when choosing a college?**

_____

_____

_____

# College Vocabulary Quiz

The correct answers are in *italics*.

**1. What is a scholarship or grant?**

*a. Money that you "win" or get from the government that is not required to be paid back*

b. Money given only by private colleges to help with tuition

c. Money that must be paid back immediately after college graduation

**2. What is a loan?**

a. Money from a bank that does not have to be paid back

b. Money borrowed only from family or friends

*c. Money that is required to be paid back with interest*

**3. What is work study?**

*a. Part of the financial aid package that students often earn through a job on campus*

b. Any part-time job on a college campus

c. A part-time job you get college credit for doing

**4. What are placement tests?**

a. Tests to determine what college you go to based on your interests and skills

b. Tests to determine your place in the freshman class

*c. Tests of your skills that will determine whether you must take remedial classes in college*

**5. What are remedial or "developmental" classes?**

a. Classes to help you prepare for college

*b. College classes that you must take and pass, but for which you do not receive college credit*

c. Classes to help develop your social skills

**6. What is the Common Application?**

*a. A single application that can be used to apply to more than one college*

b. An application that is accepted at every college and university in the US

c. An application to perform with the rapper Common.

**7. What is FAFSA?**

a. A major offered at some private universities

*b. A form that you must complete to be eligible for financial aid*

c. A diet that insures that you will not gain 15 lbs in your freshman year

**8. What is an associate's degree?**

a. A four-year degree

*b. A two-year degree*

c. A five-year degree

**9. What is a master's degree?**

*a. An advanced degree in a specialized field, like business or social work*

b. A degree earned in four years

c. A degree from a large university

**10.** Match the following **college costs** to their definitions.

a. Room
b. Board
c. Textbooks
d. Travel
e. Health insurance
f. Fees
g. Misc

1. Extra costs, like lab or copying fees for some classes
2. The cost of food, such as a meal plan
3. Insurance which some colleges require you to pay
4. The rent for your dorm room or apartment
5. The cost of buying all of your books for classes
6. Movies, concerts, snacks, clothing, etc.
7. The cost of getting to and from school

97

# College Application Calendar

What do you need to do to get into college, and when? In your small group, put a chart like this on the board or on a couple of flip charts. Then take your set of "college activity cards" and tape them in the chart in the order that you think they need to be done.

**Junior Year**—Fall semester

_____

_____

**Junior Year**—Spring semester

_____

_____

_____

_____

**Summer** (July/August)

_____

**Senior Year**—Fall semester

_____

_____

_____

_____

**Senior Year**—Spring semester

_____

_____

# College Application Calendar (completed)

Here is a completed college application calendar. Note that this is an "ideal" calendar. If you are currently entering your junior year of high school or are younger, this may work for you, though you still may not be able to take every step (such as visiting colleges). Also note that there are many other things you can or should do, like talk with an adult who has been to college, but this gives an overview of some of the key dates and activities.

If you are older, remember that there are many paths to college, including starting college as an adult. For example, you can enroll at a community college to get back in the swing of school. Community colleges often don't require SATs, letters of recommendation, etc. You just have to graduate from high school or get a GED and complete the college's application. Many other colleges have programs for adults, too.

**Junior Year**—Fall semester

- Sign up for and take the PSAT.
- Start thinking about which colleges you might want to apply to. A meeting with your school guidance or college counselor can help you figure out where to start.

**Junior Year**—Spring semester

- Ask your counselor about free or low-cost SAT prep classes, and take one if you can.
- Sign up for and take the SAT.
- Call any colleges in your area that you might be interested in, and ask about taking a tour of the campus.
- Take advantage of any college tours offered by your school or other organizations.

**Summer** (July/August)

- Make a list of schools you want to apply to. Research them at www.collegeboard.com or in college books at the library.

**Senior Year**—Fall semester

- Sign up for and take the SAT again.
- Complete your college applications for schools with fall or winter deadlines.
- Ask teachers, mentors, or supervisors to write recommendations for you.
- Research scholarships and start applying for any that you are eligible for.

**Senior Year**—Spring semester

- Fill out your FAFSA form and apply for other financial aid (ask your counselor for help).
- Complete your college applications for schools with spring deadlines.
- Your final step is to review your acceptance letters and decide which school to attend, based on their academic program, the cost, and other factors that are important to you.

Sign up for and take the SAT again.

Start your college applications.

Sign up for and take the PSAT.

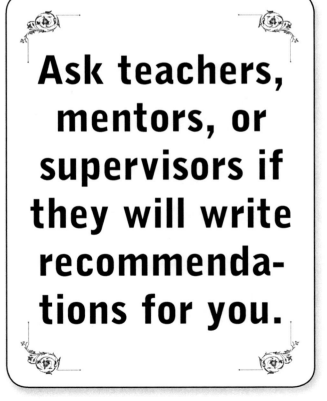

Ask teachers, mentors, or supervisors if they will write recommendations for you.

Fill out your FAFSA form and apply for other financial aid (ask your counselor for help).

Complete college applications for schools with fall/winter deadlines.

Complete college applications for schools with spring deadlines.

Review acceptance letters! Decide which school to attend.

Research scholarships and start applying for any that you are eligible for.

Ask your counselor about free or low-cost SAT prep classes, and take one if you can.

Call colleges in your area that you might be interested in, and ask about taking a campus tour.

Start thinking about what colleges you might want to apply to. Meet with your college counselor.

**Sign up for and take the SAT.**

**Make a list of schools you want to apply to.**

# You're the Admissions Officer!

You are a team of college admissions officers for one of the colleges listed below. The students on the next page have applied to your college. Your job is to admit students who are likely to succeed at your college. (You cannot just admit someone and hope they will succeed.) Who do you accept for your school? Make your choice and then write the reasons for your selection on the chart that follows.

## Ivy Hill

This is a very selective school. It gives equal weight to SAT scores and grade point average (GPA), but it has discovered that students with combined SAT scores of below 1,900 rarely succeed there. It also gives a fair amount of consideration to extracurricular activities, but only those in which the teen has had a strong, longstanding leadership role, or in which the teen has demonstrated top talent (such as first violin in the school orchestra).

## City Tech

This school is designed to be a first step for students who have not done well in high school, but who have now decided that they want a college education. It does not require SAT scores, but of the students who are admitted, the average combined score is 1,200. The average GPA of admitted students is 2.5. (The school does not consider extracurricular activities or letters of recommendation in making its decision.)

## State U

This is a large, competitive state university. Because it gets so many applicants, most of them are screened in or out based on just two factors: grades and test scores. Ninety percent of the students admitted have a GPA above 2.75 and combined SAT scores above 1,600. However, 10% of students (who have lower grades and test scores) are admitted based on other factors, such as being very good athletes or exceptional musicians, or having overcome significant obstacles, such as growing up in poverty or being recent immigrants (but even these students usually must have SAT scores above 1,450 and a GPA of 2.5 or above).

## Private Place

This small, private college accepts a wide range of students and works hard to get a student body that is diverse by geography, race, income level, interests, and talents. It is expensive, but it provides good scholarships and work-study jobs for poor and lower-middle-class students, which can make it as affordable as State U for some students.  Because the school is small, it wants each student to bring something special, so it places special emphasis on talents like sports or arts, leadership, and a demonstrated ability to get along well with others. Average SAT scores range from 1,500 to 1,800, but many students score lower or higher. The average GPA of admitted students is 3.25.

## CANDIDATE 1

- Has a 3.0 (B) grade point average (GPA)
- Got a 1,400 on her SATs
- President of the student council at her high school
- Plays on the school's volleyball team, but not good enough to play in college
- Strong letter of recommendation from the assistant principal and two teachers at her high school
- Wrote a college essay about her leadership experience on the student council, but the essay was not very well written

## CANDIDATE 2

- Has a 2.5 GPA (B-, C+), but grades got significantly better in junior and senior years
- Got a 1,525 on his SATs
- Attended three high schools (moved foster homes)
- Did not particpate in extracurricular activities (never got settled in one school)
- College essay was not strongly written, but clearly showed how the writer had learned to cope with challenging situations while changing schools and foster homes

## CANDIDATE 3

- Did not take the SAT
- Did not graduate from high school
- Got a 2,900 on the GED (pretty high score) at age 20
- Has worked for two years in a community-based teen filmmaking program and has created a film about three friends who had babies as teens
- Strong recommendation letter from the director of the film program
- College essay describes how she blew off school until she realized she was going nowhere, then studied like crazy for the GED. Claims she's now ready to be a serious student

## CANDIDATE 4

- Has a 3.8 (A) GPA
- Got a 2,200 on his SATs and similar scores on three SAT II (subject) tests; scored 3 or higher on five Advanced Placement exams
- Wrote for the school newspaper for two years; worked tech crew for school plays for three years
- Strong college essay confirmed the student's interest in college
- Strong letters of recommendation from several teachers, including newspaper advisor and theater director

## CANDIDATE 5

- Has a 2.2 (C-) GPA
- Got a 1,200 on the SATs
- Worked up to 20 hours per week throughout high school
- Participated in some intramural sports

# The Admissions Committee Report

| College & Criteria | Students admitted or rejected, and why. |
|---|---|
| **Ivy Hill**<br><br>SAT: 1,900 or higher<br><br>GPA: 3.75 or higher<br><br>Extracurriculars | Admitted:<br><br><br>Rejected: |
| **State U**<br><br>SAT: 1,600<br><br>GPA: 2.75<br><br>Plus 10% for other reasons | Admitted:<br><br><br>Rejected: |
| **City Tech**<br><br>HS diploma or GED<br><br>Does not consider extracurriculars | Admitted:<br><br><br>Rejected: |
| **Private Place**<br><br>Many factors, including diversity | Admitted:<br><br><br>Rejected: |

# My Plan for Applying to College

**1. Three careers I'm interested in:**          **Major or degree I will need:**

_____          _____

_____          _____

_____          _____

**2. Name of a college graduate I can talk to:** _____

**3. Three questions I can ask him/her:**

_____

_____

_____

**4. Test dates:**

Month I can take the PSAT _____

Month I can take the SAT _____

Month I can retake the SAT (if necessary) _____

Other tests, if any, that are required or recommended by the schools I am applying to:

☐ SAT IIs      ☐ AP Tests      ☐ Portfolio

**5. Things I can do to prepare for this test:**

This week: _____

This month: _____

In the next few months: _____

_____

**6. Colleges or universities I want to learn more about:**

_____          _____

_____          _____

**7. Name of an adult I know who can help me with the application process:**

_____

# Education Pays

Following are examples of three career fields—nursing, teaching, and bookkeeping—where increasing your education almost always leads to substantial increases in your salary.

**Nursing:** The lowest paid job in this chart requires a high school diploma and a few months of specialized training. As you go up the chart, a four-year college degree is required (bachelor's), then a graduate degree (master's), and/or specialized training and certification.

| | |
|---|---|
| **Certified Nurse Assistant** | $24,500 |
| **Licensed Practical or Vocational Nurse** | $33,500 |
| **Nurse Practitioner** | $60,000 |
| **Nurse Anesthetist** | $100,00 - $160,000 |

**MORE EDUCATION**

**MORE $$$**

**Teaching:** Teacher's aides often need only a high school diploma or two-year degree, while teachers usually have a bachelor's degrees, and administrators usually must have master's degrees. (Note: Teacher salaries vary widely in different communities around the country, but it is almost always true that the more education the educator has, the higher the pay.)

| | |
|---|---|
| **Teacher's Aide** | $17-$25,000 |
| **Starting Teacher (New York City)** | $42,500 |
| **Principal (New York City)** | $135,000 |

**Business:** Bookkeepers generally do not need college degrees, while accountants must have a bachelor's degree.

| | |
|---|---|
| **Bookkeeper (typical starting pay)** | $22,000 |
| **Accountant (first year)** | $40,000 |

Sources: PayScale.com, NYC DOE Salary Schedules, and others.

# SESSION 6: CAREER EXPLORATION

## From Job...to Career

# Rewriting My Dream

## Story & Workshop Summary

**Time:** 180 minutes (including one 15-minute break)

**Materials:** chart paper, markers, pens, sticky name tags, chart for "Resumes 101" activity, signs for "Steps to a Career that Works" activity, tape

**Story:** Rewriting My Dream

**Core Emotions:** desire to please one's family, fear, confusion, excitement, fulfillment

**Theme:** What you want for yourself in the future may be different from what your parents want for you. In the end, you need to find the best fit for your goals and talents.

**Plot:** As a member of an immigrant family from Haiti, Marsha's early career goal is to become a doctor. But by the middle of junior year, she discovers a passion for writing. Becoming a doctor symbolizes success to her parents, but becoming a writer is something she wants to do.

## Youth Development Goals:
• Young people will be able to define the difference between a job and a career.
• Young people will identify their own career goals and will begin to plan the steps they can take starting now to help them achieve those goals.
• Young people will increase their understanding of the purpose and components of a resume, and complete a sample resume of their own.

*Note: It is a good idea to review group guidelines at the beginning of each session.*

 **Opening Icebreaker**

**Who Am I?** (10 min)
**guess the job**

In advance of the session, prepare a stack of sticky name tags, each with the name of a job written on it. These should include jobs that participants are likely to be familiar with, and might include things like cashier, nurse, bike messenger, bus driver, teacher, lawyer, or doctor. Distribute one name tag to each participant, and instruct participants to stick the name tag on the back of another participant *without* showing it to him or her.

Each participant should go around the room asking yes or no questions that will help them figure out the job on their back. If anyone has a hard time guessing, participants can give each other clues until everyone has guessed correctly.

• Debrief: Did anyone have a job they'd never heard of? Was the job something they'd consider doing in real life? Why or why not?

## Read the Story and Talk About It (20 min)

**Introduce the story:** Tell the class that you are going to read a story about a girl who is considering two different career paths: one that would please her family and one that would be a better fit for her interests and talents.

**Take turns reading the story:** Take turns reading the story. Pause from time to time when there is a passage that you think is ripe for discussion. Ask the suggested questions, or add ones that you think will be helpful to your group.

Walter Moore

# Rewriting My Dream

**By Marsha Dupiton**

1. Entering my 1st grade classroom that day felt exhilarating. Everyone had come to school dressed as what they wanted to be when they grew up. Decked out in a custom-tailored lab coat and a pin that said "Dr. Marsha Dupiton," I felt superior to the ballerinas and firefighters gathered inside my classroom. I was shy and usually the last to do anything. But that day I made sure I was first in line to present my future career to my parents and the rest of the world.

   When the music was cued, I strutted across the stage and twirled twice to show off my costume. I caught the eye of my mother and heard the cheers of my aunts, and right then and there I was sure of what I wanted to be when I grew up. If I got a standing ovation for dressing up as a doctor, then I would really be celebrated if I actually became one.

91

**Q.** Why would her family celebrate her choice to be a doctor? What do you think their reaction might have been if she had dressed up as a ballerina or a firefighter?

## REAL JOBS

### 2. Family Pressure to Be the Best

I had chosen that costume because of my own doctor. Whenever I went for a checkup, he would use his secret weapon to loosen me up: his Daffy Duck and Bugs Bunny impersonations. He would ask what I was doing in school and was always interested in what I had to say. He seemed so important, yet humble, and I wanted to be just like him. I could imagine helping my patients, young and old, to feel as good as new.

As I got older, I became more serious about my career choice. I took an interest in science experiments and worked hard in science class. My parents quickly latched onto the idea. When anyone asked what I was going to do when I grew up, my family members, close and distant, would say, "Marsha is going to be the family's first doctor."

> **What mother doesn't want to say to her friends that her daughter is a doctor?**

My parents had moved here from Haiti in their early 20s, along with my grandparents, aunts, and uncles, to get a better life for themselves and their future children. My cousins and I were to reap all the benefits of their sacrifices. My father always said to my sister and me, "You're lucky you were born in the United States because you get so many opportunities. Take advantage of it!"

Among my family members, we had a boatload of future professions: a doctor, a lawyer, a pharmacist, and don't forget your traditional nurse. There was so much pressure to become the best.

### 3. I Was Pegged as the Future Doctor

My science grades weren't Einstein-worthy—at the start of high school, I was getting C's in science, compared to A's and B's in my other classes. But that didn't stop me from imagining my future as a doctor.

**Q.** Do you think she "owes it" to her parents to become successful? Why or why not? How would they define success?

92

*Finding Your Path*

I would have a huge office, three phones that rang off the hook, and a chic condo in Manhattan that I would rarely see because I'd be working and traveling so much. Helping others was still part of my motivation, but I also wanted to be rich and successful and have a job that was practical. Then, one day in the middle of 9th grade, everything changed.

"Marsha? Can you please come see me for a second?" asked Mr. James, my English teacher, during class one day. I looked up from my book, puzzled. Had I heard him right? As far as I knew, a student was only called to the teacher's desk because they were bad or disrupting a class. But I'd done all my work. In fact, our last assignment was one that I'd worked hard on and really enjoyed. I'd written a short story about a girl starting high school for the second time because she moves around a lot.

4. **Writing for Fun?**

I got up and slowly approached his desk. Right foot, left foot. Head down. "Yes?" I said. He slid my 10-page story face-down toward me, his face blank as a canvas.

I picked it up quickly to get it over with. My eyes grew wider each time I blinked at the grade in red on my cover page. An A? I'd hoped for a B or even a B+, but an A, that left me speechless.

"Your story was incredible. There was a lot of description and it seemed as if I was there. Did you ever think of writing something other than for a grade?" said Mr. James.

I shook my head, thinking, "Why would I do that?" Then Mr. James told me he would look for writing programs for me, and that he wanted to display my story on his bulletin board. I was proud that someone had acknowledged my success in one specific thing rather than the general compliments I got on my grades as a whole. For the first time, I was great at something in particular instead of pretty good at everything. I went home that night, pulled an old composition notebook from my bookshelf, and started writing for fun.

Writing all my feelings and thoughts on paper was something

93

**Q.** Why is being a doctor practical? Why is practicality important to her?

**Q.** Is it better to be very good at one particular thing or somewhat good at lots of things? Why?

## REAL JOBS

entirely different from preparing to become a doctor. Writing made me feel free.

5. **A New Dream**

As my English grades continued to shine, I began to imagine what it would be like to be a writer, how it would make me feel happy like it did now. But it seemed far-fetched to me, like a fairy tale job. So I kept my love of writing to myself.

Whenever someone asked what I wanted to be, I still said, "A doctor." But by the middle of junior year, there was no excitement in my voice anymore. I realized that I'd wanted to become a doctor because it symbolized success. I'd been attached to getting the prize, but not the work that was before me for years to come. Becoming a doctor was no longer my dream, but a roadblock to my passion: writing.

I wanted a career that incorporated writing and informing people about environmental issues. That's when I thought of becoming a journalist. It was like a ready-made job for me. So when I found out about a rigorous summer journalism workshop last spring, I eagerly grabbed an application.

6. **Breaking the News to Mom**

Then I sat in my room trying to muster the courage to tell my mother about it. I didn't think my father would mind my change in plans too much, but my mother would be harder to win over. What mother doesn't want to say to her friends that her daughter is a doctor? Finally I picked up the application and walked toward the kitchen, where my mother was preparing dinner.

"Hey Mommy, I have a thingy to do in the summer with writing. I think it would really help me out senior year," I said quickly. I tried to make my face look blank but failed terribly. She took the application and started to read.

"What is this? You want to be a journalist? What about becoming a doctor? Why would you want a profession that pays so little and has so much competition for jobs?" she said.

94

**Q.** What does she mean when she says writing seems far-fetched? How do you think her parents would react if she told them she wanted to be a writer instead of a doctor?

*Finding Your Path*

"I just really like to write and you know how I've always excelled in English class. This workshop is to improve my writing. If I'm not cut out for it then I'll turn back to becoming a doctor!" I said. But this was a lie. I knew that I would do great in this program. Getting that application was fate.

"You better know what you want; college is around the corner," she said. Her face was drawn and she seemed confused. But she didn't say no.

I walked out of the room feeling that somehow I'd won the battle. I filled out the application right away and put it in my bag.

> **For most of my life I never felt I could do something unpredictable.**

**Q.** How important is it to know what you want to do for a career before you go to college? What would happen if you changed your mind halfway through college? What would happen if you changed your career choice after graduating from college? What would happen if you changed your career choice after working in a particular career for ten years?

Later that night, I overheard my mother on the phone with my aunts, saying, "Marsha wants to be a journalist now. I just hope she doesn't become like her cousins who bounce between different majors and colleges each year."

I felt frustrated because I'd finally told her about my passion and she didn't fully understand. I've never flip-flopped in my decisions or ideas and I've always been serious about my future.

7. **What If I Failed?**

On the other hand, I understood her concern. She felt that becoming a journalist left much more room to fail than becoming a doctor would. And I felt the same way.

When I got an acceptance letter from the summer journalism program a week later, it was an eye opener for both my mother and me. To be chosen out of 50 applicants for only 10 spots reassured my mother that I wasn't going to dive into an occupation that I didn't know I would do well in.

During the writing workshop, my mother did a complete 180. She took an interest in my writing, asking about my day and when my stories were going to get published so she could read

**Q.** Why does her mom think that journalism leaves more room to fail? Do you think she's right about that? Is that a reason to avoid it?

95

## Real Jobs

them. I feel relieved and happy because it would be a lot harder without her support.

My mother isn't the only one who has changed; I have too. For most of my life I never felt I could do something unpredictable. Becoming a doctor was like a ladder. First college, then medical school, and then a residency. But the paths to becoming a writer are less clear. I'm not sure if there are enough jobs for writers, or whether they pay enough to live comfortably. That made me feel uneasy at first.

8. **My Pathway to Happiness**

For my family, like those of many immigrants, unpredictability isn't an option. Our elders made sacrifices to give us the best of everything here, and we're supposed to become successful so we can give back to them and our native country. I still feel that pressure to be the best for my family and for myself.

But it's different this time around. Now that I'm doing something I truly love and know I'll do well in, not just something that puts extra money in my pocket, I feel less pressured and afraid about my choice.

Journalism feels like a more mature and realistic career choice for me than medicine. Even though it's not exactly what my family had in mind for me, I feel that journalism is my pathway to my own personal happiness and success. And at the end of the day, that's what matters most.

---

*Marsha was 17 when she wrote this story.*

**Q.** Is it better to have a high-paying career that you don't really like or a lower-paying job that you love?

# Explore the Ideas

### Discussion: When I Grow Up (10 min)

Ask the Group:
• When you were little, what did you want to be when you grew up?
• Did your family or friends know? What did they think?
• Do you still have the same goal now? If not, why did you change your mind? Do you think you'll change your mind again someday?

### Activity 1: What Should Marsha Do?
**worksheet, pair share, share out** (15 min)

Ask participants to work in pairs to complete the worksheet on p. 22, "What Should Marsha Do?" [Leader's Guide p. 121]. Give them about 10 minutes to work on it and then ask the pairs to share their responses with the large group.

Ask:
• What kinds of factors influence a person's career choices?
• Which factors are the most important? Why?

### Activity 2: Jobs versus Careers
**large group discussion** (10 min)

Ask participants if they know the difference between a job and a career. Explain that while the terms "job" and "career" are often used interchangeably, there are important differences between them. On a flip chart, write the following:

Job: $ for right now, experience
Career: what I want to do long term, satisfaction

Present the following ideas, either by facilitating a discussion and guiding the group to them with your questions, or by reading or paraphrasing.

*Jobs are for the short term.* They are often a means to an end. You need to help pay for your college tuition, so you find a part-time job at a restaurant. Or you take on a summer job at the mall to earn spending money. Or maybe you get a job after college through a temp agency to help pay the bills. Sometimes jobs lead to careers.

*A career is something that you build during your lifetime.* Career planning is the ability to look ahead and think about what's important to you, where you want to go and the steps you need to take to get there. Research shows that the careers that make people happiest are ones that provide three things: a fit with your talents, pleasure, and meaning. So, for example, if you are detail-oriented, enjoy working in an office with lots of people, and have strong faith, then a job as an administrator in a religious institution would probably be a good fit for you. But if you aren't detail-oriented, that job could be tough no matter how much pleasure or meaning it provides. Building a career unfolds over a lifetime as you improve your skills and education, learn more about yourself and what you like, and discover new opportunities.

### Activity 3: Steps to a Career that Works (for You)
**social barometer** (25 min)

*Note: Before the session begins, you should post the signs for this activity around the room.*

Ask participants to stand in the center of the room facing outward and look around at the signs that list several different career fields. There should be one sign for each of the following career fields:
• Business

- Civil Service/Government/Law
- Military/Law Enforcement
- Trades/Blue-Collar Jobs
- Technology
- Health Professions
- Education
- The Arts

*Tip: Try to post the signs so that similar career fields are close to one another. For instance, Civil Service/Government/Law should be near Military/Law Enforcement.*

Explain that these are just a few examples of possible career fields they might be interested in. Tell them you are going to read a series of statements to them, and ask them to follow the directions as you read them. At the end, see where they end up and discuss.

### Civil Service/Government/Law

- If you are interested in doing work that provides vital services for the public, take a step toward the sign.
- If you are interested in working for a city or federal office (post office, sanitation, fire department, etc.) take a step toward the sign.
- If you are interested in working on policy issues that affect the United States and the world, take a step toward the sign.
- If you are interested in studying and understanding the law, take a step toward the sign.

### Military/Law Enforcement

- If you are interested in being a cop, soldier, or FBI agent, take a step toward the sign.
- If you would like a job with clear rules, discipline, and order, take a step toward the sign.

### The Arts

- If you are interested in writing or journalism, take a step toward the sign.
- If you like fine arts, such as painting or drawing, take a step toward the sign.
- If you are interested in performing arts,

such as acting or drama, take a step toward the sign.
- If you are interested in producing or creating movies or music, please take a step toward the sign.

### Technology

- If you are interested in creating new and innovative products, please take a step toward the sign.
- If you like computer programming or working with computers and/or electronic products, take a step toward the sign.

### Health Professions

- If you are interested in being a nurse, doctor, or physical therapist or working in another area of health care, take a step toward the sign.
- If you have always had a passion for helping people heal and can see yourself working in a hospital or related health-care institution, take a step toward the sign.

### Education

- If you see yourself working with children in the future, take a step toward the sign.
- If you have a passion and want to help educate children, take one step toward the sign.
- If you're good at explaining new concepts and ideas to other people, then take a step toward the sign.

### Business

- If you would like to start your own business—and are willing to work long hours to make it successful—then take a step toward the sign.
- If you like accounting, working with numbers, learning about investing, or economics, then take a step toward the sign.
- If you have worked for someone else and are constantly thinking about how to make the business run better, then take a step toward the sign.

## Trades/Blue-Collar Jobs

• If you would like a career that requires specialized training but doesn't require a college degree, like electrician, plumber, or bus driver, take a step toward the sign.

• If you like to work with your hands, take a step toward the sign.

• If you are "mechanically inclined" (interested in fixing things and in how things work), take a step toward the sign.

Once you've read all of the statements, ask participants to turn to someone standing near them and talk about where they're standing. What career did they move toward? Were they surprised at all by where they ended up?

Discuss with the large group:
• Do you think where you ended up is a good indication of the career that's right for you? Why or why not?

Reiterate that these are just a few examples of career fields they might want to pursue. Explain that there are not hard and fast lines between one careers and another. There are many careers that combine elements from more than one of these categories and many jobs that fall into more than one career category. Remind them that the career choices they make are not limited to the categories on the walls. There are hundreds of careers they have never heard of that they might learn about down the road. It is up to them to blaze their own path and to explore their options.

*Note: The workbook page titled "Helpful Websites for Teen Job Seekers" includes a suggestion for a possible extension activity. Between today and the next time you meet with your group, suggest that the teens use these websites to research jobs they're interested in. Ask each teen to come back to the next session with at least one job they found in their research.*

**Break** (15 min)

## Activity 4: Resumes 101

**discussion** (20 min)

Ask if anyone knows what a resume is. Have students read aloud "Resume Basics" on p. 23 in the workbook [Leader's Guide p. 122]. Then review some of the things that are commonly found on resumes, using the sample resume on p. 24 of the workbook [Leader's Guide p. 123]. Here are some points to make as you go through the sample resume with students:

• **Contact Information:** Make sure to include your name, address, and current phone number and an appropriate, professional email address.

• **Experience:** Anything you've done that has helped you build skills. (This doesn't have to be paid employment. It can include internships, volunteer work, or other experience that is related to your job search like babysitting or mowing lawns.)

• **Education:** The name, city, and state of your high school and date of expected graduation. If you are currently enrolled in college, include that information as well. (If you are out of college, do not include your high school information on your resume). You can also include your GPA if it is 3.5 or higher and any academic awards or honors you've received.

• **Skills:** Things you can do. This section can include any special skills you have that are relevant to the jobs you are applying for, such as such as typing, filing, or copying; computer programs you know how to use; or foreign language skills. It can also include skills like how to use machinery or tools. If you're good at public speaking, list "presentation skills." Don't exaggerate, but don't be shy about what you already can do. You could also list generic skills, like "CPR certification."

## Activity: Group Resume
**worksheet, sharing, group writing, share out** (50 min))

Ask each participant to independently complete the Resume Worksheet on p. 25 in the workbook [Leader's Guide p. 124]. Give them about 10 minutes to work.

When time is up, break participants into groups of four or five. Give each group a sheet of chart paper and a marker. Tell them that they now have 15 minutes to create a resume based on their *collective* interests, experience, skills, and education. They will present the resumes and you will "hire" the group that presents the best one.

Everyone must contribute something to the resume based on group members' *real* qualifications (jobs they've held, volunteer work, babysitting, skills, etc.). They will also have to give their "candidate" a name and fictional contact information including an appropriate email address.

When time is up, give each group a chance to present their candidate's resume to the larger group. Congratulate all of the groups. Then pick the winner who you will "hire."

# Closing Activity (5 min)

Ask each participant to complete this sentence: **"One thing I can do now to help prepare for a career that will work for me is…"**

# What Should Marsha Do: Be a Doctor or a Journalist?

In the story "Rewriting My Dream," Marsha (the author) struggles with her choice to pursue a career as a writer rather than pursuing her childhood dream of being a doctor. In the space below, write what you think are the pros and cons for Marsha of each of those two career choices.

| PROS | |
|---|---|
| Reasons Marsha should become a doctor: | Reasons Marsha should become a journalist: |
| Total Pros       Doctor: _____ | Journalist: _____ |
| **CONS** | |
| Reasons Marsha should NOT become a doctor: | Reasons Marsha should NOT become a journalist: |
| Total Cons       Doctor: _____ | Journalist: _____ |

Look at the number of pros and cons for each career. Do you think they reflect the best choice for Marsha? Why or why not?

# Resume Basics

**What is a Resume?**

A resume (pronounced REH-zuh-may) is a summary of your employment history, plus some information about your education and other experience or talents (like the ability to speak a second language). The idea is to select specific parts of your experience that demonstrate that you can do a particular job well. The resume is often the main tool employers use to screen job seekers, so in order to get an interview, you need a solid resume. (You may also need to include a cover letter or complete an application.)

The most common resume includes your contact information, a list of the jobs you've held starting with the most recent one, your education, and a brief list of other talents or activities.

**A Few Simple Things to Keep in Mind**

**KEEP YOUR RESUME TO ONE PAGE**. As a young person with a relatively short work history, you should keep your resume to one page. Shorter resumes are often harder to write, but when you do them properly, they pay off; in most cases, a busy employer will not read a resume that is longer than one page.

**KEEP THE DESIGN SIMPLE**. A resume should be clear, not creative. Your resume should be neat and should follow a traditional format. It should be printed in black ink on white or off-white paper. Do not use fancy typefaces.

**BE HONEST**. Employers check the information you list on your resume. If it's not accurate, you will not be considered.

**MAKE SURE YOUR RESUME IS ERROR-FREE**. A typo or other mistake on your resume will often disqualify you. Ask an adult with good proofreading skills to carefully review your resume.

## Kevin Jones
87 Washington Street
Flushing, NY 11233
(718) 555-5555
kevinjones@webmail.com

## EXPERIENCE

July - Aug 2008     **Literacy Help Center, Brooklyn, NY**
*Tutor*

- Assisted children ages 6-7 with the fundamentals of reading and math

Sept - Dec 2008     **Jefferson High School English Department, New York, NY**
*Office Assistant*

- Performed various administrative duties to support department staff, including typing and filing

- Attended weekly staff meetings; compiled and distributed meeting minutes

Oct - Dec 2007     **Habitat for Humanity, Flushing, NY**
*Volunteer*

- Worked with other volunteers to paint, install windows, and clean house for needy family

- Recruited others to participate in the rebuilding project

July - Aug 2007     **City Children's Services Day Camp, New York, NY**
*Counselor in Training*

- Worked with Lead Counselor to plan activities for a group of 10 fourth-graders

## EDUCATION

**New York City High School**, New York, NY
Expected Graduation, June 2010
Dean's Honor Roll

## SKILLS & INTERESTS

- Proficient in Microsoft Word
- Fluent in Spanish
- Type 40 WPM
- DJ for parties and school events
- Can design simple web pages

# Resume Worksheet

## Contact Information

Name: _____

Address: _____

Phone number: _____
If you expect to be called back by an employer, your phone message must be brief and professional with no music

Email: _____
If you don't have one, create a professional email address like this: your.name@yahoo.com

## EXPERIENCE

List three things you've done that count as experience (even if you've never had a job):

1. Name of company/person, city, state: _____

    What you did: _____

2. Name of company/person, city, state: _____

    What you did: _____

3. Name of company/person, city, state: _____

    What you did: _____

## EDUCATION

Your school: _____ Date you expect to graduate: _____

City and state: _____

## SKILLS & INTERESTS

List two skills you have (including computer skills and any foreign languages you speak):

1. _____    2. _____

## Honors/Awards

List any honors or awards you've earned:

_____

## Extracurricular Activities

List any hobbies or activities you participate in that you think employers might want to know about:

_____

# SESSION 7: REFLECTION

## Looking Back and Moving Forward

# Growing Up On the Job

## Story & Workshop Summary

**Time:** 180 minutes (including one 15-minute break)

**Materials:** chart paper, markers, pens, M&Ms, chart with color key for "You've Got Skills" activity, copies of the cards for "Networking for Success" activity

**Story:** Growing Up On the Job

**Core Emotions:** determination, self-control, a sense of responsibility, shyness (overcoming)

**Theme:** Work can help you grow as a person.

**Plot:** The author gets her first job at age 15 and finds that working teaches her how to be responsible, stay cool under pressure, and overcome her shyness.

## Youth Development Goals:
• Young people will identify the skills and knowledge they have gained as a result of working.
• Young people will identify some goals and how their work experience to date can help them achieve those goals.
• Young people will define and practice "networking" and will gain tools that will help them make and keep professional contacts in the future.

**Note:** *It is a good idea to review group guidelines at the beginning of each session.*

## Opening Icebreaker

**Group Snapshot** (15 min)
snapshot pose

Break participants into groups of four or five and ask them to talk briefly about their work experience so far at their current jobs. Ask:
• What is one skill that you have learned?
• What is one thing you have learned about yourself as a result of working?
• What was the best moment at work and worst moment at work so far?

Ask each group to choose one "best" and one "worst" to share with the larger group.

Tell them they are going to create a photograph that captures the best experience they've had on the job so far. They need to decide what the event or scene is, and who is in the picture. Once they have their scene and character, ask them to work together to create a "snapshot" of the moment by standing together and posing. Their goal is for the rest of the group to be able to guess what is happening in the "picture." Give the groups a few minutes to create their snapshots and then let each group present. Ask the audience to guess what's being depicted, then give the groups a chance to explain.

## Read the Story and Talk About It (20 min)

**Introduce the story:** Tell the class that you're going to read a story about one young woman whose job experiences have helped her in many ways.

**Take turns reading the story:** Pause from time to time when there is a passage that you think is ripe for discussion. Ask the suggested questions, or add ones that you think will be helpful to your group.

Ora Obhas

# Growing Up On the Job

### By Josbeth Lebron

1. Having to ask your parents for money has to be one of the most annoying things there is. They'll never just give it to you—they always want to know what it's for and why. Since you're not enjoying that line of questioning, you begin wishing you had a job. I know this for a fact because it's what started me on my first job search when I was 14.

   At the time, I assumed that if I had working papers and a place was hiring, then they had to give me a job. I was wrong. I went from clothing stores to supermarkets and none would hire me because of my age and lack of experience. I tried to look for a job at least four times that year, in different sections of Queens and Brooklyn, but no one would hire me.

   I was 15 by the time I finally got one. Luckily, my gym teacher had taken my constant complaints about how much I needed a job seriously. So, when he heard about something called The Big

67

**Q.** What are some reasons it might be hard for young people to find jobs? What other kinds of jobs could Josbeth have looked for as a 14-year-old (e.g., babysitting)?

**Q.** What are some of the reasons it might be hard for young people to find jobs? What other kinds of jobs could Josbeth have looked for as a 14-year-old (e.g., babysitting)?job that you love?

**Q.** What makes Josbeth good at this job?

**Q.** What skills do you think she developed at her first job that might help her do well in this job? Discuss the concept of "transferable skills," or skills that you can use in many different settings and that aren't specific to one particular job.

---

### REAL JOBS

Apple Games, he told me where to get the application.

The Big Apple Games is a program that allows teenagers and children to use school facilities over the summer for recreational purposes, like sports and arts and crafts. It also sponsors competitions between schools. I applied and got a job at my school's pool, helping autistic and mentally ill children learn how to swim.

2. **My First Job: Great but Temporary**

Those kids made the job a wonderful experience for me. They seemed so frightened and curious and needed to have someone around them constantly in order to feel comfortable and protected in the water.

One little girl would only dunk her feet in the water and would not dare to go in completely. I always offered to carry her into the water but she would refuse, even though I could see the curiosity in her eyes.

Finally, toward the end of the summer, she made the decision to go in, but only if I would carry her. That day we had so much fun. Instead of playing with all of the kids I dedicated my time to her. Whenever she got scared she would clutch her arms around me. I was so proud of her because even though it took her some time, she somehow built up the courage to go in the water.

That was a great job except for one thing—it was temporary. In August, I was on the prowl again. One night a friend of mine who worked at the Metro Mall in Queens, New York told me that a bagel shop was hiring. I went there the next day and they hired me on the spot just because I had worked before. It didn't even matter that my summer job had nothing to do with bagels. They must have been in desperate need of a worker.

3. **From Bagels to Videos—for Peanuts**

I learned how to make sandwiches, serve ice cream, work the register, and make coffee and tea. It was fun but I was only there for a month because the owner decided to sell the place, and the

68

---

new owner brought in his own employees. Still, it was something to add to my resume.

After a short vacation, I went into a neighborhood video store and asked if they were hiring. They told me to come back on the weekend, so the boss could interview me. I went back on a Saturday morning and they put me right to work (they called it "training"). They hired me mainly because I had experience working a register.

I had to organize the movies, sell greeting cards, and work the register. The work wasn't bad but the job had problems. First, I had to work the whole weekend, from morning till late at night, so I had no time to go dancing or to the movies with my friends. And since it was off the books, they paid me a lot less than minimum wage. I was working excruciating hours for just a few peanuts.

I stayed there for three months only because I was too lazy to go out and find something else. What got me out of there was a family emergency that required a trip to Puerto Rico. I was there for a month, which was longer than expected. When I returned I decided not to go back to the video store.

> I assumed that if I had working papers and a place was hiring, then they had to give me a job. I was wrong.

**Q.** What skills did Josbeth learn that month? Was this job a success or failure? Why?

4. **Dressing for Success**

Instead, I went and got an application at a shoe store that was being remodeled. Three days after turning in the application, I was hired. That was a year and a half ago and I'm still there.

My jobs have taught me a lot. You'd be amazed what you can learn just working in a shoe store. For one thing, in the workplace rules are enforced, and this has taught me to be responsible. I have to be at my job on time and dressed from head to toe in proper attire (meaning slacks or a skirt, a blouse, and dress

**Q.** Ask if anyone knows what "off the books" means. Explain or elicit: It's when the employer pays cash. You can avoid paying taxes, but you don't get any benefits, like unemployment, disability, social security, etc.

69

REAL JOBS

shoes).

If I didn't dress in that manner then I would get written up, and after three write-ups I'd get fired. Lucky for me I haven't been written up yet. I guess it's because I understand the importance of the dress code. I receive more respect from elders when I'm well dressed and make a better first impression on customers.

**Q.** Is it fair that she has such a strict set of rules to follow?

Another useful skill you learn in the workplace is how to communicate. You have to know how to speak to people, whether it's over the phone or in person. You must always keep a positive tone. Let's just say a customer needs your help to find a certain shoe, and you don't think you have it. You don't say, "We probably don't have any more." Instead you have to say, "Sure, I'll check to see if I can find it." You always have to be polite. If you're not, you'll be sure to have some problems with your boss.

> **You'd be amazed what you can learn just working in a shoe store.**

5. **Extreme Patience Is Required**

Many times you will find yourself in a position where you really don't feel like being nice. That's when patience and self-control come in handy—two more qualities I've developed at my jobs. For example, one time I had been going nuts all day, helping people find what they wanted. Some couldn't find a certain style in their size, others wanted their feet measured, and the rest were driving me crazy by asking me the same questions over and over. "What's the price on this?" (It's right in front of their faces.) "Is it on sale? Why not?" I was totally exhausted and frustrated.

Then, on top of all that pressure, I got one customer who approached me with a nasty attitude and told me he wanted a certain shoe. I told him, "OK, just hold on one moment until I finish helping her." He responded, "Just hurry up 'cause I ain't got all day for this #@!#@."

**Q.** How could Josbeth respond to this and still keep her job?

70

*Managing Your Time*

I wasn't even gone for a minute when I heard stacks of shoe boxes falling from the overhead racks where we store the stock that doesn't fit on the shelves. The guy had decided he didn't need me and tried to get the shoe himself; instead, all he did was make a mess.

To top that, he left that mess on the floor and walked out without buying anything. I was the miserable one who had to pick it all up. And all I could do was curse the man out in my head when I really felt like beating him up with the shoes.

6. **Working Brought Me Out of My Shell**

But I kept cool. I released my frustrations by discussing the situation with one of my coworkers. They always seem to find a way to help me laugh at these incidents. One of my friends said, "What a herb, maybe he thought they would give him a job if he got the shoes himself. Too bad he flunked training." Another guy said, "Did you see how fast he ran? He probably thought we were going to kick his ass. What a wuss!"

Comments like that never cease to amuse me. It's even funnier when we have to whisper to each other so the manager can't hear us. On this particular occasion even the customer I was helping before I was so rudely interrupted joined in.

Working has also helped me improve my social skills. I used to be the type of person who never spoke unless I was spoken to. But having to talk to complete strangers at work all the time has changed me. Sometimes I find myself smiling at people on the street just because I woke up in a good mood. On the train I'm no longer afraid to comment to someone about how beautiful a day it is if that person looks friendly enough to listen. Working really does help relieve shyness.

7. **No Free Time, But No Regrets**

The only drawback is that I feel as though I have rushed my teen years just to be independent. I never have time to hang out at the mall, go Rollerblading, or just hang out with my friends,

**Q.** Ask the group to describe a situation where they supported or got support from a coworker. Why did they do it? How did it feel?

71

REAL JOBS

because I'm always too busy working. My friends don't even invite me anywhere anymore because they know I won't have the time to go. I miss hanging out but I don't regret working.

So if you're in need of some cash or you have some spare time left between school and homework, my best advice is: Get a job! It's not that hard, all you have to do is keep looking. Don't give up just because a couple of people turn you down. If you do get that job, expect to sacrifice plenty of playtime. But in the end you'll find it's worth it.

*Josbeth was 17 when she wrote this story. She graduated high school and attended Baruch College.*

**Q.** Do you think it was a mistake for Josbeth to focus so much on working and less on her friends? What are the advantages in the short term? In the long term?

72

132

# 🔍 Explore the Ideas

## Activity 1: Your Work Experience
### freewrite, discussion (20 min)

*Note: This activity assumes participants are working. If they are not, rephrase the questions to ask what it has been like to read and discuss the stories and participate in the activities in the* Real Jobs *program.*

Ask participants to freewrite on their work experience using the following prompt. Read the prompt aloud and then give participants 90 seconds to write their responses.

*What has working been like for you so far? What have you enjoyed about it? [Pause]*

*What has been challenging? [Pause]*

*Imagine that it is the same time next year. What are you doing? How has your experience working this year helped you to reach new goals?*

When time is up, ask participants to turn to a partner and share one thing they wrote. Then give participants the opportunity to share their response(s) with the large group. No one has to share if they don't want to.

Ask: "How do you think your work experience so far may benefit you in the future?"

Ask: "Why is it important to take the time to reflect on your work experience?"

Elicit that, like Josbeth does in the story, it's important to reflect on what you've gained from working—the skills, the insights about what you like and don't like, and what you're good at—because knowing those things will make it easier to get your next job.

Briefly review "Moving Forward—Steps for Finding Your Next Job" on workbook p. 27 [Leader's Guide p. 139].

## Activity 2: You've Got Skills!
### game, pair share, share out (20 min)

*Tip: Before class, post a flip chart with the color key and the definitions of the words (see below), so it's ready when you start the exercise. Or, as you're setting up the activity, have a teen with good handwriting copy the information below onto the flip chart.*

Pass around a bag of M&Ms and instruct each person to take five but DO NOT eat them (yet). Then ask each participant to find a partner. Explain that they will tell their partner one thing about themselves for each piece of candy in they've selected, and that each color represents something different, as explained on the flip chart.

• Green: Job Skills (things you are good at/ new skills you've learned from working)

• Red: Knowledge (things you've learned as a result of working)

• Blue: Interests (things you are interested in/new interests you've developed as a result of working)

• Yellow: Experience (something about your job experience that you think will help you in the future)

• Orange: Career Objectives (things you hope to accomplish in your future career)

For instance, if a person has three green candies and two blue ones, they would have to share three job-related skills and two interests that they have.

Give participants 10 minutes to share, and then debrief with the large group by asking volunteers to share some examples of the skills, knowledge, interests, experience, and career goals of their peers.

**Break** (15 min)

## Activity 3: "I Commercial" worksheet, pair share, share out (15 min)

Explain that it is important to be able to speak about yourself and your experience in order to help you make professional contacts, including potential future employers. It's also important in job interviews to be able to answer one of the most commonly asked (but surprisingly tricky) interview questions: "Tell me a little about yourself." They need to answer in a way that is appropriate for a job interview. Ask for a volunteer or two to try answering the question on the spot.

[If necessary, give them an example. If a new friend asked that question they might say that they're a short, funny, Aquarius who loves Chinese food and playing the drums. But they would tell an employer that they're honest, punctual, have good typing skills, and have passed a class in Microsoft Office.]

Point out that it can be difficult to respond to this question if you're not prepared. Tell participants they're now going to create an "I Commercial"—a 30-second introduction of themselves.

*Tip: Consider creating and sharing your own "I Commercial" as a model for the group.*

Tell the group they will have 10 minutes to work independently to complete the "I Commercial" worksheet on workbook p. 26 [Leader's Guide p. 136]. When time is up, ask everyone to find a partner and practice sharing their "I Commercials" with each other. After a few minutes, ask for volunteers to share their commercials with the larger group.

## Activity 4: Networking for Success game (30 min)

*Note: Copy and cut out the Networking for Success cards before beginning the activity [Leader's Guide p. 137-138].*

Ask the group to define the term "networking." Explain that networking is a process of meeting new people and developing professional contacts. These are people who might be able to help you move ahead in your career. It's important to note that networking is a two-way street. Your professional contacts are there to support you, but you can also support them. For example, if they are looking to fill a job that's not right for you, you can connect them with someone you know who would do well in that position.

Give each participant one of the Networking for Success cards. (You can make up your own in addition to the ones that are included here.) Tell participants that their objective is to *become the character named on their card*, and to meet the other people in the room while playing the role of that character.

If their character is looking for something, they should try to find someone who can help them. Remind them that even if they meet someone who can't help them, they should try to find a way to be helpful to that person. (This is a good way to create good professional relationships in the long term.)

Tell participants they have 10 minutes to introduce themselves and talk to as many people in the room as they can (without rushing through the interactions too much). When time is up, ask everyone to take a seat.

Debrief:

   • What stood out about this experience? Did you get help? Were you able to help anyone?

## Activity: My First Job, the Movie
### brainstorm, role play (40 min)

As a large group, ask participants to think of some of the challenges they've faced in their work experience so far. Record their responses on chart paper. Referring to some of the items on the chart paper, ask participants to describe how they were able to overcome those challenges.

Break participants into small groups of three or four and tell them they are directors who need to produce a movie trailer for an upcoming film. The hero of the movie is a young person who has just gotten his first job. The plot of the movie should show this young person facing some of the challenges on the list you just made. The plot should also show how that character responds to those challenges, and how he or she (hopefully) overcomes them. It should also include some specific examples of things this character gains as a result of working. Encourage them to be as dramatic as they'd like.

They should give their film a title, and everyone in the group should play an active role in the production. Give the groups about 15 minutes to work, and then give each group a chance to share their trailer with the large group.

## Closing Activity (5 min)

Ask each participant to complete this sentence: **"One thing I've learned or gained from working that will help me in the future is…"**

# "I Commercial"

One of the most commonly asked interview questions is "Tell me a little about yourself." This may seem like an innocent question, but it's not. Learning how to answer it is one of the deep secrets of doing well in an interview so you can get that job. You're going to answer the questions below and then create a 30-second "I Commercial" that will help you ace that question.

1. Who are you? (This is more than just your name. It's how you identify yourself to an employer. For example, "I'm a junior at Anytown High School," or, "I'm an English major at City College.")

2. What career field do you work in or what field are you trying to break into?

3. What experience have you had that is relevant to your goal?

4. What did you learn or what skills did you gain through that experience?

5. What are you looking for now (a chance to schedule an informational interview, an internship or job, etc.)?

**Now, put it all together. Here's an example:**

"Hello, I'm Deirdre Smith. I'm a senior at Wonderful High School. I'm interested in a career in education. I just completed a summer internship at a nonprofit organization called Read for Success, where I tutored middle school students who were having trouble with reading. I learned techniques for helping them improve their reading skills. I am very interested in a job in your afterschool program. I think I could use some of the skills I learned in the internship in your literacy program. I am also eager to learn new skills. Could I send you my resume or come in for an interview?"

You're an employer at a computer company who is looking for an unpaid summer intern who is bright and eager to learn.

You're an employer at a magazine publishing company who is looking for someone to do some part-time office work.

You're a doctor looking for a full-time receptionist.

You're a journalism major in college looking for an internship.

You're a medical student trying to decide which type of medicine you should specialize in.

You're an English major in college who is looking for a part-time job to make some extra money

You're a high school student who is looking for his first part-time summer job.

You're a teacher and you know of a job opportunity answering phones in the main office at the school where you work.

You're a high school student who wants to become a doctor one day

You're a high school student who loves to write and wants to learn more about jobs that involve writing.

You're a business owner who needs help in the office but can't afford to pay an employee.

You're a high school graduate who is looking for work in an office

You're a summer camp director who is looking for a full-time summer counselor.

You're a high school student who is interested in working with children. You have to take one or two summer school classes.

# Moving Forward—Steps for Finding Your Next Job

**Step 1: Decide what you're looking for.**

To land the job you want, you first need to think about what's important to you in a job. Ask yourself:

- Are you willing to take an unpaid internship for the experience?
- How much do you want to earn?
- What locations would you be willing to work in? (Can you get there?)
- What type of environment are you looking for (e.g., an office, outdoors, working with children, etc.)?

**Step 2: Figure out where to look.**

There are many places teens can look for job openings, so take advantage of all of them. Good resources include:

- Friends, family, neighbors, teachers, and other people who know you
- Local businesses, especially those with "help wanted" signs in the window
- Classified ads in places like craigslist, other online job sites, and community newspapers
- Community bulletin boards
- The career center at your school

**Step 3: Network!**

Talking with people who can help you in your job search is called networking. Think about who you can ask for help, such as:

- Parents, family members, or family friends
- School career counselors, guidance counselors, or teachers
- Previous employers
- Friends.

**Step 4: Apply.**

- If you've never filled out a job application before, make a copy of the application and practice first. Then have someone check it over.
- Remember to have your resume ready and obtain working papers if you're under 18 years old.

**Step 5: Follow up.**

Keep track of the jobs you're applying for and make a plan to follow up to show your interest.

- Keep track of the names of the people you speak to if applying for jobs in person. When submitting your application, tell them you'll stop by in a week to follow up, and then remember to do it!
- When applying online or by email, try to find the name of the person you are sending your application or resume to. A week or so after you apply, send a follow-up email to express that you're still interested in the job.
- Always remember to send a thank-you note after any job interview.

# Self-Evaluation

If you have completed most or all of the sessions in the *Real Jobs* program with your students, they have undoubtedly made substantial progress in learning what it takes to be successful on the job. If they have simultaneously been working, in a summer job or co-op program, for example, they have probably made even more progress.

However, because most of the learning has been through experiential activities, they may not be aware of how much they have learned.

For a quick review of what students have learned, ask them to complete the activity sheet "Advice for Job Seekers and New Hires" (right, and p. 29 in the student workbook). As the instructions make clear, students are to think back to their first day on the job, or to the day they started the *Real Jobs* program in your class.

Remind them that there are many things they didn't know about work and the working world that they they now know — from reading the stories, participating in the activities, and working, if they are in a work program.

They should make use of their new-found knowledge to give "advice" the the person they were at the beginning of the program about how to succeed at work. For example, they might tell the person that being punctual is more important than they imagine, or that employers don't expect you to know everything and want you to ask for help. They should write about what most stands out for them.

It is easy to tear out page 29 in the workbook. We encourage you to have students write their "advice" and hand it in to you. You'll learn a lot about what they got out of the program. If possible, collect and record their "evaluations" before the last class. Then, on the last day of class, report back to them some of the "advice" they gave, and compliment the entire group on learning so much.

You might even want to compile a list of "peer advice" about the world of work, based on these evaluations, that you can share with subsequent groups.

## Another Evaluation Idea

*Real Jobs* includes seven stories, and more than two dozen activities and worksheets. Some are bound to work better with your group and your teaching style. If possible, use 45 minutes in a class near the end to ask the participants which activities worked best for them, and why. Then ask which ones they liked least, and why. (You may want to copy the table of contents from this Leader's Guide to have in front of them during the discussion so they can refresh themselves on the stories and the activities.)

Then use the information from the discussion to improve the workshop. You can spend more time on the most effective activities, or modify or eliminate the ones that don't work for your group.

# Advice for Job Seekers and New Hires

Don't put your name on this sheet. When you're done, tear it out and give it to the workshop leader.

Think back to your first day on the job. There are probably some things you know now that you wish you knew then. Based on what you've learned since then, what advice would you give yourself about how to succeed at work? Give yourself at least three pieces of advice.

_____

_____

_____

_____

_____

_____

_____

_____

_____

_____

_____

_____

_____

_____

_____

_____

_____

## *About Youth Communication*

Youth Communication, founded in 1980, is a nonprofit youth development program located in New York City whose mission is to teach writing, journalism, and leadership skills, and to make youth voices heard as widely as possible. Each year, 100 public high school students write and illustrate Youth Communication's two award-winning teen magazines. The writers are a diverse group, including teens in foster care, recent immigrants, and low-income youth. Working with full-time professional editors, the writers may take several months to complete a single story. This process results in writing of uncommon depth and authenticity. The true stories in this anthology were written by teens in the Youth Communication writing program.

In addition to publishing magazines, Youth Communication has published more than 70 anthologies on topics teens consider most important, such as peer pressure, families, and improving their communities. Stories by teens at Youth Communication are also frequently reprinted in popular and professional magazines.

Youth Communication strives to serve three primary audiences: teen writers, teen readers, and educators.

• Writers: Writing for peers motivates teens to develop their literacy skills, meet deadlines, think critically about their experience, take individual responsibility, and work as a team to produce high-quality magazines.

• Readers: Teen readers report that reading their peers' stories makes them feel less isolated and more hopeful about the future. They also say that the stories give them information they can't get anywhere else and promote discussions with parents and other significant adults.

• Educators: Teachers and youth workers use Youth Communication publications to inspire reluctant readers and to broach difficult topics in safe and stimulating ways. They also report that reading our books and magazines shows them what's really important to teens, which helps them establish better relations with their students and clients.

**Youth Communication ®**
224 W. 29th St, 2nd Fl.
New York, NY 10001
212-279-0708
www.youthcomm.org

## About Development Without Limits

Development Without Limits is an educational consulting organization that supports youth development programs and schools developing curricula, training staff, and working directly with young people. Since it was founded in 2000, Development Without Limits has worked with hundreds of community-based organizations, afterschool and summer programs, schools, and other educational institutions, and thousands of young people.

The mission of Development Without Limits is to provide dynamic and challenging learning experiences for young people and adults alike. The philosophy of Development Without Limits is based on the idea that people learn best and are most productive when they are interested and engaged in what they are doing, and when learning itself feels meaningful. For this kind of engagement to occur, activities need to be dynamic and based upon the skills, interests, and ideas of the participants. Development Without Limits approaches each project as something new, tailoring programs, curricula, and staff development to meet the unique needs of each organization.

Development Without Limits has co-created curriculum for youth on topics including work readiness, conflict resolution, global literacy, and more. DWL conducts dozens of staff development workshops each year on topics such as Positive Discipline, Child and Youth Development, Group Management, Project-Based Learning, Activity Planning, and more.

Development Without Limits provides professional development in how to implement the *Real Jobs, Real Stories* program. For information, contact:

**Development Without Limits**
16 W. 32nd St. #10J
New York, NY 10001
212-244-4351
www.developmentwithoutlimits.org

# *About the* Real Jobs *Anthology*

The activities in the *Leader's Guide to Real Jobs, Real Stories* are based around stories by teens about work and related topics that appear in the *Real Jobs* anthology. In addition to the seven stories that appear in the Leader's Guide, the *Real Jobs* anthology includes another 26 stories by teens about their work experiences.

The anthology can be used in conjunction with this Leader's Guide. Or, if you are not running a program but would like to give teens a book in which peers explore a wide range of work experiences, you can order the anthology separately. Here is the table of contents of the *Real Jobs, Real Stories* anthology

# *The Real Stories Program*

Real Stories is the umbrella name for a series of programs that promote reading, social and emotional development, and the knowledge and skills young people need to succeed. The program is aimed at middle and high school students—especially those who are resistant to reading. The entire series is built around true stories by teens in the Youth Communication writing program. The stories are paired with experiential activities that reinforce the themes of the stories.

The first program in the series, *Real Stories, Real Teens*, focuses on general themes of youth development and identity. It also promotes extended reading through the inclusion of novels from the Bluford series. *Real Stories, Real Teens* is designed to be used in out-of-school time settings like after-school and summer programs. It is also suitable in some school settings, like advisories or classes where teens are very resistant to reading. It consists of an anthology with 26 true stories by teens and three fiction excerpts, a detailed Leader's Guide with 28 experiential workshops, and a dozen Bluford novels. Real Stories, Real Teens won the 2008 award for best curriculum in its class from the Association of Educational Publishers.

The second program in the series, *Real Jobs, Real Stories*, is focused on work readiness for teens. It is designed to help teens find and succeed in their first jobs. The Real Jobs program consists of an anthology of 33 true stories, an extensive Leader's Guide, and a 32-page workbook. The Leader's Guide includes 21 hours of experiential workshops with dozens of activities.

The third program in the series, *Real Men* (available in 2011), will focus on the experiences of young men of color and the struggle to figure out what it means to be a man. It will include an anthology of true stories, an extensive Leader's Guide, and a short film on DVD about one young man's journey from dropping out to professional success.

\* \* \*

Reading the stories in the Real Stories program, talking about them with peers, and engaging in the activities from the Leader's Guides helps young people explore ideas and values, engage in healthy discussion, and reflect on their own lives and choices.

In many of the stories, the writers describe how they coped with significant challenges. The activities in the Leader's Guide help teens imagine how they would manage similar challenges (or avoid them in the first place). The activities also show teens how they can be helpful and supportive of their peers.

A key benefit of the Real Stories program is that it makes reading an enriching and rewarding experience. Unlike traditional reading programs, Real Stories engages hard-to-reach teens by providing them with peer-written stories that are engaging and model good choices and values. That helps build teens' motivation to read, while strengthening their skills.

## About the Writers and Editors

**Rebecca Fabiano** is the vice president of capacity building for the Philadelphia Youth Network and a consultant for Development Without Limits. From 1999 to 2006, Rebecca was the founding director of Opening Doors and Building Bridges, a youth development and after-school program in New York City. Rebecca was a 2003 Robert Bowne Foundation Fellow. She is an adjunct professor at The Community College of Philadelphia and teaches a course on youth work.

**Eric Gurna** is the founder and executive director of Development Without Limits. He previously served as director of staff development for LA's BEST After School Enrichment Program in Los Angeles, where he co-founded the LA Partnership for After School Education. Prior to that, Eric worked for Educators for Social Responsibility and Rheedlen Centers for Children and Families (now Harlem Children's Zone). He received a master's degree in urban policy analysis and management from the New School for Social Research.

**Keith Hefner** co-founded Youth Communication in 1980 and has directed it ever since. He is the recipient of the Luther P. Jackson Education Award from the New York Association of Black Journalists and a MacArthur Fellowship. He was also a Revson Fellow at Columbia University. He has written and tested curriculum that accompanies Youth Communication's teen-written books and magazines for more than 20 years.

**Andrea Kamins** is the associate director of Development Without Limits. She provides staff development, technical assistance, and other supports to youth development programs nationwide. Andrea has worked with young people ranging from pre-K through college. She earned her bachelor's degree in psychology from Oberlin College.

**Laura Longhine** is the editorial director at Youth Communication. She edited *Represent*, Youth Communication's magazine by and for youth in foster care, for three years, and has edited several Youth Communication anthologies. She has a bachelor's degree in English from Tufts University and a master's degree in journalism from Columbia University.

**Sam Quiah** is a senior consultant with Development Without Limits. He leads trainings, provides technical assistance, and develops curriculum to support out-of-school-time programs. He was formerly the project director of the Human Rights Activist Project with Global Kids. Prior to that, he worked at the Asian American Legal Defense and Education Fund and at South Asian Youth Action (SAYA!). He has a master's degree in social work from Columbia University.

CPSIA information can be obtained at www.ICGtesting.com
Printed in the USA
LVOW021440030112

262203LV00001B/53/P

9 781933 939971